The American Society of International Law

STUDIES IN FOREIGN INVESTMENT

AND

ECONOMIC DEVELOPMENT

Previously published

Foreign Enterprise in India: Laws and Policies by Matthew J. Kust

Foreign Enterprise in Colombia: Laws and Policies by Seymour W. Wurfel

Foreign Enterprise in Nigeria: Laws and Policies by Paul O. Proehl

Supplement to **FOREIGN ENTERPRISE IN INDIA**

Supplement to FOREIGN

ENERPRISE IN INDIA

Laws and Policies

By MATTHEW J. KUST

THE UNIVERSITY OF NORTH CAROLINA PRESS · CHAPEL HILL

Foreword

In 1964 Mr. Kust's *Foreign Enterprise in India: Laws and Policies* was published, the first of several studies of the legal environment for foreign investment in selected countries written under the auspices of the American Society of International Law. That study examined the principal institutions of law, legislation, and administration affecting foreign private investment in India in the context of underlying economic policies, political development, and social change.

Mr. Kust's initial volume dealt with these developments during the period of India's independence roughly through 1963, with historical background for perspective. Since that time there have been important new developments in the legal and administrative framework for investment in India. The present volume is a valuable supplement examining changes in the two and a half years that have passed since the earlier work was completed.

The new study, like the others in the Society's program (on Colombia, India, Japan, Mexico, and Nigeria), was prepared under a research fellowship from the Society. The Society has been able to assist in the preparations of these useful volumes as a result of a grant from the Ford Foundation, whose interest and support we want gratefully to acknowledge. The statements of facts and expression of opinions are the responsibility of the author.

H. C. L. Merillat
Executive Director
American Society of International Law

Washington, D. C.
October, 1966

Contents

Supplement to FOREIGN ENTERPRISE
IN INDIA

I

Historical Background

The death of Jawaharlal Nehru in May, 1964, afforded India a first chance to demonstrate to itself and to the outside world the vitality of its democratic institutions. With discipline and facility, the majority Congress party elected a new parliamentary leader, Lal Bahadur Shastri, who became the second prime minister of India. Succeeding a towering figure of history like Jawaharlal Nehru as head of a democratic nation of 485 million people was a formidable undertaking. Moreover, India's persistent crises—food shortages, lack of foreign exchange, population growth, and others—seemed more intractable than ever during 1964 and 1965. By the autumn of 1965, however, the humble and self-effacing Shastri attained great political stature, largely through his handling of the war with Pakistan. In fact, he had already started to demonstrate political boldness in accepting the resignation of his controversial finance minister, T. T. Krishnamachari, a Nehru holdover, on December 31, 1965, and the concessions, unpopular with many of his countrymen, he made at Tashkent in the greater interest of peace in South Asia. His untimely death at Tashkent in January, 1966, as the result of a sudden heart attack, was unfortunate for India.

Once again, however, the succession was executed smoothly. This time the Congress party took a somewhat surprising, certainly unusual, step in electing as prime minister a woman, Indira Gandhi, the daughter of Jawaharlal Nehru. Mrs. Gandhi, whose competence has already been demonstrated, will probably require a year or two to acquire the necessary political stature for effective administration. This is not peculiar to India but characteristic of all democratic successions, whether under the parliamentary or presidential systems. It was unfortunate for India, however, to have to pass through two such periods in quick succession while it was confronted with difficult problems of social and economic development.

Mention must be made in this context of Kumaraswami Kamraj, the president of the Congress party. Mr. Kamraj became a powerful factor in Congress party politics after, and even before, Jawaharlal Nehru's death. He might have sought the premiership himself and, perhaps, might even have secured it. Unfortunately certain limitations would have handicapped him as head of state in India; he has no fluent knowledge of English or Hindi and has had no international experience. He chose, therefore, to stay in the background and pilot the Congress party caucuses through the difficult tasks of selecting the new prime ministers. It was Kamraj who was mainly responsible for developing the party consensus for both Shastri and Indira Gandhi; the result of an efficient political machine in action. It might be in order, thus, to requote the prescient words of Woodrow Wyatt, who said, in 1962, "When the time comes for Nehru to depart, Cabinet government will emerge more vigorously. There will be a slight shift to the right, both nationally and internationally and Nehru's successor will not be selected by himself but by the Congress caucus, which has the most efficient political machine in any democracy in the world, including America."[1]

II

Economic Planning

The Fourth Five-Year Plan for the period April 1, 1966, to March 31, 1971, proposes to extend and accelerate the pace of industrialization of the country. The highest priority is given to production of fertilizers, insecticides, agricultural tractors, implements, pumps, and related items required to increase agricultural output. Almost equal priority is extended the efficient and accelerated development of the capital goods industries with the view of increasing the export of manufactured articles as the long term solution of the balance of payments problem. The remaining priorities are tempered to support and foster these two major objectives.

The minimum financial outlay is predicated at 21,500 crores ($45.15 million) with 14,500 crores to be invested and expended in the public sector and 7,000 crores in the private sector. Power, transport, communications, and industry will absorb 12,100 crores. Agriculture and irrigation are allocated 4,100 crores. The balance will go toward education, health, housing, and other social development.

Formulation of the final plan has been delayed because of the uncertainty over foreign aid. It is, however, expected that the final plan will be ready before the end of the fiscal year 1966-67. An interim one-year plan has been provided for the first year of the Fourth Plan.

Indian policy makers and planners are often accused of allocating insufficient resources to agriculture and overemphasizing industrialization. The conclusion is then drawn that this is the reason for the periodic food shortages in the country. This is a dubious criticism, inconsistent with experience elsewhere, particularly in America, which has attained the highest degree of agricultural productivity in the world. America's leap forward in agricultural productivity dates back a mere twenty-five years after the country attained a high level of industrialization, which enabled it to apply the benefits of industry—mechanical power, improved farming implements, chemical fertilizers, pesticides, and herbicides—to agricultural production. In view of this experience in America and other industrialized countries, industrialization and the application of its benefits to agriculture is viewed as the ultimate solution of the food problem in India. The Memorandum on the Fourth Five-Year Plan states, "The development of agriculture . . . is closely linked with the development of power, transport and industries. . . . The supply of fertilizers, pesticides, construction materials, implements and processing equipment required for the success of the agricultural programme . . . would depend upon an appropriate expansion of the industrial sector."[1]

In addition to greatly increased fertilizer and pesticide production, the plan hopes to achieve self-sufficiency in the establishment of fertilizer and pesticide factories. The tremendous increase in steel production and machine making achieved by the end of the Third Plan now makes this possible. The manufacture of tractors and agricultural implements is already on a self-sufficient basis. Therein is contained the hope of the solution of the food problem in India. It is the heart and core of the Fourth Plan.

Moreover, agricultural production capacity has risen substantially since the First Five-Year Plan from 50 to 90 million tons of foodgrains. Substantial though the increase has been, it is insufficient to meet the burgeoning demand generated by population growth and increased incomes arising from new employment opportunities under the plans. It is the latter, actually, that provides the greatest demand for food as the newly employed, emerging from a low economic level, are prone to spend most of their increased incomes on more and better food. Hence, the pressure on wheat and rice. When the rains fail every five years or so, the loss of food production results in serious to acute food shortages. But this situation in India will not be overcome until the country industrializes so that the attributes of modern industry can be effectively applied to agricultural production.

The Fourth Plan is heavily dependent on foreign economic assistance. According to the memorandum on the Fourth Plan an aggregate amount of Rs 4,000 crores of gross external assistance will be required, of which 1,350 crores are needed for interest and repayments on prior loans. The net assistance of 2,650 crores, when compared with the figure of Rs 2,100 crores for the Third Plan—which was only one half in magnitude—indicates a diminishing dependence on foreign aid.

The prospects for such external assistance are reasonably good. If the consortium of western countries maintains about the same net inflow attained during the Third Plan and the Soviet bloc does the same, the requirement would be met. This would mean, however, some moratorium or postponement of the payments burden on the old debt. The additional amount needed can, perhaps, derive from the international finance institutions such as IDA and the proposed Asian Development Bank. A substantial inflow may also be derived from foreign private investment.

Export earnings during the Fourth Plan are expected to total Rs 5,100 crores, predicated, hopefully, on an intensified export drive, but maintenance imports, including components needed for the manufacture of industrial machinery and transport equipment, have been estimated to total Rs 5,300 crores. External assistance will, therefore, be required to maintain the existing industrial capacity at full production. This is doubtless one of the major problems of economic planning in India at this time. It results from a deficiency in planning, though not entirely. Complex industrial machinery and transport equipment cannot be produced completely from the start. The difficult components take several years of learning before they can be produced. The production of metals, chemicals, and other industrial requirements has not kept pace. The import of metals in excess of Rs 150 crores in 1964-65, mostly iron and steel, could have been eliminated through better planning of the fourth steel plant or some other source of steel production.

Self-sufficiency in industrial production and vigorous promotion of exports of manufactured goods will receive great attention during the Fourth Plan. Export promotion will be discussed subsequently. It is not generally recognized how close the country has moved toward self-sufficiency in various industrial areas during the Third Plan.

India manufactures all its railway transport requirements, with the exception of diesel and electric locomotives for which about 50 per cent of the components are imported. It is planned to reduce these imports to 20 per cent by the end of the Fourth Plan. Wagons and coaches are now being planned for export.

Automobiles are produced indigenously to the extent of 80 per cent; trucks and buses to the extent of 90 per cent. It is expected that automotive equipment will be produced completely in another two years.

About half of the machine tool requirements are made indigenously. This is expected to rise to 75 to 80 per cent during the Fourth

Plan. Electric power equipment—turbines, boilers, transformers, and switchgear—is expected to derive entirely from domestic manufacture by the end of the Fourth Plan. Diesel engines, electric motors, pumps, and similar items are already being produced in sufficient quantities.

During the Fourth Plan, India expects to enter the final phase of industrialization; that is, self-sufficiency in establishing its own basic industrial plants. By the end of the Fourth Plan, the country expects to be 75 per cent self-sufficient in establishing new steel plants, and the sixth steel plant, during the Fifth Plan, is expected to be handled entirely by Indian engineers and supplied with machinery and equipment of domestic manufacture. Similar competence to establish refineries and fertilizer plants is to be developed by the end of the Fourth Plan. The latter is to be stressed particularly as the ultimate solution of the food problem.

If the pace of industrial growth of the past decade continues and the foregoing expectations of self-sufficiency are fulfilled, India will be a fully industrialized nation based around a steel capacity of about 25 million tons by 1975. Thereafter, it will be able to rely on its own resources, human and physical, for continued economic growth.

The Third Plan ended with mixed results. Food production fell considerably short of the 100 million tons target for food-grains. The last year of the plan, 1964-65, suffered the worst monsoon failure in half a century. The actual food production was therefore no true measure of the country's productive capacity. It is estimated at about 92 million tons, still considerably short of the plan target. Intimately associated with this failure was the shortfall in nitrogenous fertilizer production by 350,000 tons. The reliance upon the private sector and foreign investment failed to materialize. The reasons are too complex and controversial for detailed analysis here.

On the other hand, the basic industrial targets were attained in most cases and exceeded in some. There was some loss of time in steel plant expansion with the result that the 9 million ton capacity will not be reached before 1966-67, a year later.

Electric power capacity also lagged but rose from 5.6 to 11.7 million KW. Cement capacity exceeded the target by a million tons. Aluminum fell short by 7,000 tons. Locomotives, coaches, and wagon production achieved plan targets, as did most categories of industrial machinery. Machine tool capacity reached its target. There was a shortfall in the production of commercial automotive vehicles, largely because of lack of imported components. The most serious failure was in alloy and special steels.

The development of basic industries under the Second and Third Plans was substantial. Steel capacity increased from 1.74 to 9 million tons—a record matched by few, if any, countries in their economic history. Electric power generating capacity increased from 3.4 to 11.7 million KW. Machine making and allied production showed a similar three or fourfold increase in production during the period.

In sum, the Third Plan took the country to the threshold of self-sufficiency in important areas of industrial development. The Fourth Plan is designed to attain self-sufficiency or near self-sufficiency in most industrial sectors.

The major obstacles persist. The foreign exchange shortage is serious and will not be alleviated until industrial self-sufficiency is attained, and exports of manufactured goods are greatly increased. Substantial progress is expected in both respects under the Fourth Plan. External assistance of the magnitude set forth above will be necessary and vital to alleviate the foreign exchange shortage.

The food shortage can be expected to persist for at least another decade. India will need outside supplies of food when the rains fail periodically, to prevent inflation and famine. This may be more difficult to obtain henceforth on the same favorable terms as America has worked down its agricultural surpluses. Much will depend, therefore, upon the decisions in Washington in the next few years.

Population control remains intractable though not ignored. Successful development, more specifically the health programs, requires a constant adjustment of population projections upwards. The latest estimates put the population projections at 495 million in 1966, 560 million in 1971, and 630 million in 1976. "One of the most important tasks of the Fourth Plan will be to organize a concerted drive to control the growth of population through family planning," states the Memorandum on the Fourth Five-Year Plan.[2] Rs 95 crores is provided for a broad program of birth control. Even the private sector is being enlisted through tax concessions for expenditures on promoting family planning among its employees.[3]

A difficult decade is, therefore, in prospect. The strain on resources will be acute and will require sound planning. Continued external assistance will be vital. Given these factors, it is not unreasonable to expect most, if not all, of the present problems to be considerably ameliorated in ten years.

III

Foreign Collaboration

Foreign collaboration continues strong. After attaining a high of 403 foreign collaboration approvals in 1961, the number dropped to 298 for each of the years 1962 and 1963. The decline was doubtless attributable to the Chinese aggression and the ensuing tightening of the rupee capital market. In 1964, the number rose again to 403, but declined in 1965 again to 242 for similar reasons associated with the Pakistan war. The countrywise and industrywise tabulation of approved foreign collaborations is set forth on pages 11 and 12.

The *Economic Times* has undertaken annual surveys on foreign collaboration that provide some interesting information.[1] In the October, 1965, survey, the over-all equity participation by foreign collaborators was 22.7 per cent of the issued capital. This reflects a rise from 19.9 per cent found by the survey a year earlier. In the November, 1964, survey of 131 companies involved in the 173 collaboration agreements studied, 88 had some foreign equity participation. The October, 1965, survey found similar equity participation in 38 of the 53 companies involved in the 68 agreements reviewed. The *Economic Times* surveys appear to confirm the trend toward greater equity participation over the years from mere technical collaboration of earlier years. The countrywise disposition of the degree of equity participation found by the November, 1964, survey is equally interesting (see page 13).

The sample bears out the general observation that American and British collaborators are more prone to participate in the equity of the new industrial undertaking. Japanese and German collaborators prefer to confine themselves to technical collaboration though there has been a noticeable trend toward equity participation, not reflected in the above sample, from these two countries. The October, 1965, survey

NUMBER OF FOREIGN COLLABORATIONS—INDUSTRYWISE
(Cases Approved By Government)

	1957	1958	1959	1960	1961	1962	1963	1964	1965	Total 1957 to 1965
1. Plantations	3	6	4	—	—	—	—	—	—	13
2. Sugar	4	2	2	—	—	—	1	—	—	9
3. Cotton textiles	9	4	3	2	—	1	3	—	—	22
4. Jute textiles	1	1	—	1	—	—	—	—	—	3
5. Silk & woollen	—	1	5	2	3	1	—	1	2	15
6. Iron & steel	2	—	1	1	—	—	5	38	6	53
7. Transport equipment	4	4	11	20	6	9	14	9	4	81
8. Electrical machinery, apparatus,	11	11	12	72	73	44	54	43	33	353
appliances, etc.	8	11	26	107	143	81	88	107	82	653
9. Machinery other than transport & electrical	1	1	2	1	1	1	—	—	—	7
10. Aluminum										
11. Basic industrial chemicals	5	—	4	2	3	3	4	15	7	43
12. Medicines and pharmaceuticals	4	10	9	6	3	9	2	4	5	52
13. Other chemical products	6	9	14	21	29	18	11	15	12	135
14. Cement	3	3	4	3	1	—	4	3	1	22
15. Rubber & rubber manufacturers	2	3	3	5	3	—	—	6	—	22
16. Paper & paper products	2	2	1	9	8	8	1	6	1	38
17. Electricity generation & supply	—	—	3	—	—	—	1	—	—	4
18. Trading	4	1	4	2	1	—	2	—	—	14
19. Shipping	—	2	1	—	—	—	—	—	—	3
20. Banks & Insurance	3	4	3	—	—	—	—	—	—	10
21. Others	9	28	38	126	129	123	108	156	89	806
Total	81	103	150	380	403	298	298	403	242	2358

shows equity participation of 199 lakhs, constituting 36.9 per cent, by German collaborators in 6 new Indian companies.

The *Economic Times* surveys also scrutinized the agreements for the number of foreign directors on the boards of the Indian companies. It appears that where there is equity participation the collaboration agreement usually gives the foreign collaborator the right to designate or elect one or more directors. The distribution of foreign directors is set forth below (see page 13).

About 40 per cent of the companies involved did not have any foreign directors, which accords roughly with the number having no equity participation. The most prevalent number appears to be two directors where foreign directors are provided for in the collaboration agreement.

The November, 1964, survey sets forth, most interestingly, the percentage control of the board by the foreign directors (see page 13).

FOREIGN COLLABORATION IN INDIAN
INDUSTRIES—COUNTRYWISE
(Cases Approved By Government)

	1957	1958	1959	1960	1961	1962	1963	1964	1965	Total 1957 to 1965
1. U.S.A.	6	4	10	61	77	57	67	78	48	408
2. U.K.	17	34	52	120	126	79	70	105	60	663
3. West Germany	2	6	13	58	67	42	48	68	44	348
4. East Germany	—	—	1	5	4	5	10	24	6	55
5. France	2	1	2	9	16	14	16	11	12	83
6. Italy	4	4	4	9	13	11	6	8	7	66
7. Japan	1	3	8	39	30	24	32	35	26	198
8. Sweden	1	—	1	13	—	6	1	6	3	31
9. Canada	—	1	—	1	3	6	—	3	1	15
10. Pakistan	—	2	—	—	—	—	—	—	—	2
11. Austria	—	—	1	3	5	4	2	5	1	21
12. Czechoslovakia	—	—	—	6	5	1	5	4	3	24
13. Holland	1	—	—	6	10	7	4	5	2	35
14. Switzerland	—	2	1	13	19	19	19	19	18	110
15. Belgium	—	—	2	4	2	4	3	5	—	20
16. Yugoslavia	—	—	—	—	1	1	3	2	1	8
17. Denmark	—	—	2	6	4	2	3	9	1	27
18. Finland	—	—	—	2	1	1	—	—	—	4
19. Panama	—	2	1	—	—	—	—	—	—	3
20. Poland	—	—	—	1	6	—	3	4	2	16
21. Hungary	—	—	—	1	2	2	—	3	1	9
22. Others	47	44	52	23	12	13	6	9	6	212
Total	81	103	150	380	483	298	298	403	242	2358

It would appear that majority control of the board was found in 12 of the 131 companies involved in the sample. The survey fails to reveal the extent of "effective" control, if any, that may exist in cases of 50 per cent or near 50 per cent ownership where the foreign collaborator has the right to designate the chairman with a casting vote. In sum, however, the survey reveals that the new Indian companies do not, as a rule, have foreign controlled boards.

The terms of collaboration revealed by the surveys will be discussed in Chapter VI. A few salient features of foreign collaboration may, however, be noted here.

A considerable number of multi-country collaborations were found. The November, 1964, survey contained twenty-six companies with more than one collaborator. For example, Lynx Machinery, Ltd. has five collaborators—R. A. Lister & Co., and Flexible Drive & Tool of

Country	Number	(Lakhs) Amount	Percentage
U.S.A.	27	1130	20.3
U.K.	26	602	16.9
West Germany	9	57	3.6
Japan	6	77	13.1
Sweden	5	301	54.8
Switzerland	3	55	9.7
France	3	74	13.1
Italy	2	124	18.3
Canada	2	89	18.5
Others	5	18	1.9
Total	88	2527	19.9

November, 1964 Survey		February, 1964, and October, 1965 Surveys Combined	
No. of Foreign Directors	Nos. of Companies	Nos. of Foreign Directors	No. of Companies
None	55	None	62
One	25	One	26
Two	23	Two	30
Three	13	Three	16
Four	12	Four	14
Five	3	Five	6
Total	131	Total	154

Percentage of Board	Number of Companies
Nil	55
1-10	8
11-20	23
21-30	15
31-35	3
36-40	3
41-50	12
51-60	4
60 and above	8
Total	131

Great Britain; Schiess-Defries Hebezug Und Kraubon, Gmbh and Damag Zug, Gmbh, of Germany; and Skoda of Czechoslovakia.

Majority ownership was found only in a few of the agreements. The November, 1964, survey found only 6 of the 131 companies where the foreign equity participation exceeded 50 per cent. Three companies had 60 per cent foreign ownership of the equity capital. The October, 1965, survey found a similar situation.

A major difficulty encountered by new collaborations the past few years is the tight rupee capital market. Before 1962, the rupee finance of the project gave the least concern. New equity issues where good foreign collaboration was involved were oversubscribed many times. Since 1962, finding the rupee capital for the project has become a major problem. Many collaborations have been delayed, suspended, and even canceled because of the inability to raise the necessary rupee capital.

The reasons for the poor capital market in India since 1962 are complex and unclear. It may be too glib a conclusion to attribute it entirely to the increased taxation of companies and individuals that followed the Chinese aggression, though it necessarily diminished the savings available for industrial investment. What is frequently overlooked is that the increasing tempo of industrialization has placed more capital issues on the market. This is revealed by an annual tally of new capital issues of large and medium sized companies.[2]

Year	New Capital Issues (Crores)
1956	45.1
1957	24.9
1958	25.9
1959	43.2
1960	60.7
1961	59.6
1962	73.9
1963	54.5
1964	90.0
1965	79.0

It can be seen that in addition to a heavier tax burden on its potential investors on one hand, the capital market was expected, on the other hand, to absorb more new capital issues. Moreover, there has been a heavy upsurge of building and construction for residential and commercial purposes which has absorbed crores of rupee capital that might otherwise have gone into the capital market for industrial investment. At the same time, the exuberance of the public about new capital issues that prevailed before 1962 has disappeared with the realization that the waiting period for dividends was five years or more. With all of these various factors aiding and abetting each other, a sluggish and unresponsive market has been created for new capital issues.

The government has not been callous about this pressing need of the private sector. Various tax measures have been enacted, which will be discussed in Chapter XI. The most effective step has been a strengthening of the quasi-public and public financial institutions for underwriting the new capital issues. Most notable in this respect was the founding of the Industrial Development Bank with in initial capitalization of 50 crores. The existing financial institutions, such as IFC, ICICI, and others, have been supplied with additional rupee funds. The AID Cooley loan program has been greatly instrumental in this connection by providing rupee loans on favorable terms and easing, thereby, the underwriting burden of the financial institutions in India.

While most new collaborations have been able to secure their rupee capital with such help, it has not resulted in an entirely happy situation. Unfortunately, the financial institutions have not been able to sell the new issues to the Indian public. Instead of underwriters, they have become investors. This unnatural development not only diverts and restricts them in their primary function but thrusts these public or semi-public institutions deeply into the private sector.

There appears to be no foreseeable relief of the situation. Instead the pressure on rupee capital from all quarters of the economy, attributable primarily to an increasing tempo of development, will doubtless quicken. The Government of India has made it clear that it will not permit private sector projects to founder for lack of rupee capital. Foreign collaborators must, therefore, be prepared to grapple with this problem in consort with their Indian partners for, perhaps, another decade or so.

A decade of foreign collaboration has, in general, brought forth good Indian entrepreneurship. Some of the Indian partners failed to come up to expectations. In its purpose to broaden and diversify entrepreneurship in India, the Indian government has sometimes granted industrial licenses or letters of intent to inadequate entrepreneurs. Foreign collaborators have been too prone to accept the license or letter of intent as evidence of the Indian entrepreneur's capability, only to learn later that this was not true. In general, though, the new entrepreneurs have deported themselves well. Far more have distinguished themselves than have failed.

There are two areas that the foreign collaborator would be well advised to provide for adequately in the collaboration. They are production and fiscal control, in which the new entrepreneurs are sometimes weak. Provision by the foreign collaborator of a plant or production manager and a financial controller, versed in cost accountancy, tends to shore up a new industrial undertaking at the nexus.

IV

Basic Legal Structure

The Land Acquisition (Companies) Rules, 1963, establish the procedure and rules pursuant to which a public Indian company may seek compulsory acquisition of a factory site, including land for a housing project for its workers.

A Land Acquisition Committee is required to be set up by the appropriate government (state or central government), consisting of the secretaries or other officers of the Department of Revenue, Agriculture, and Industries, and such other members as the appropriate government deems desirable.[1] One of the members is to be designated the chairman. The committee shall regulate its own procedure. It shall be the duty of the committee to advise the appropriate government on all matters relating to or arising out of the acquisition of land for a public company on which it is consulted. The advice must be tendered within one month, which may be extended to two months "for sufficient reason" by the appropriate government.

The state or central government, as the case may be, acts upon an application made by a company. Whenever such application is made, the appropriate government directs the collector (presumably in the district where the land is situated) to submit a report on the following matters:[2]

(i) that the Company has made its best endeavour to find other lands in the locality suitable for the purpose of the acquisition;

(ii) that the Company has made all reasonable efforts to get such lands by negotiation with the persons interested therein on payment of reasonable price and such efforts have failed;

(iii) that the land proposed to be acquired is suitable for the purpose;

(iv) that the area of land proposed to be acquired is not excessive;

(v) that the Company is in a position to utilize the land expeditiously; and

(vi) where the land proposed to be acquired is good agricultural land, that no alternative suitable site can be found so as to avoid acquisition of that land.

In connection with the last matter, the collector is required to consult the senior agricultural officer of the district, whether or not the land proposed to be acquired is good agricultural land. Good agricultural land is defined as "any land, which, considering the level of agricultural production and the crop pattern in the area in which it is situated, is of average or above average productivity." Garden and grove land is to be included.[3] It will be recalled that Indian agriculturists feared the loss of their land to industry, and the government assured them that good agricultural land would not be sacrificed. While the rules do not prescribe compulsory acquisition of good agricultural land, this procedural step is designed to give state governments pause for thought before acquiring the land for companies under the new power.

The collector's report must be submitted to the committee as well as the government. Before any acquisition of the land, an agreement must be entered into by the company, including the following:[4]

(1) that the company shall not use the land for any other purpose;

(2) that the time within which the factory or workers' houses shall be erected shall not exceed three years after the acquisition, which time may be extended for three successive years at a time if the appropriate government is satisfied that the company was prevented from erecting the facilities by reasons beyond its control;

(3) that the transfer may be declared null and void by the government concerned if the company commits a breach of any of the conditions provided for in the agreement with a penalty in an amount not exceeding one-fourth of the amount paid for the land;

(4) that if the company utilizes only a portion of the land for the purposes it was acquired, the transfer may be nullified with respect to the unutilized part, provided the government is satisfied it will not interfere with the use of the remaining portion by the company. The same penalty provision applies; and

(5) that any dispute with respect to the amount rebateable in connection with the unutilized portion shall be referred to the Court within whose jurisdiction the land is situated for final decision.

Another significant rule is that regarding sanction for transfer of the land.[5] The act forbids the transfer of land compulsorily acquired without the previous approval of the government.[6] Rule 8 permits such sanction only in the following cases:

(i) the proposed transfer of land along with dwelling houses, amenities, buildings or work, if any, is to some other Company or where the Company is a cooperative society, such transfer is to any or all of its members, or

(ii) where the land has been acquired solely for the erection of dwelling houses for workmen employed by the Company, the proposed transfer of the land along with dwelling houses, if any, is to such workmen or their dependent heirs.

V

Protection of Property and Business Interests

(Not Supplemented)

VI

Licensing and Regulation
of Industry

The mixed economy policy was continued by the administration of Prime Minister Shastri and it will doubtless be continued by Prime Minister Indira Gandhi. Her basic economic philosophy was set forth in an article in the *Yale Review* in 1961 in the following words:

As is generally recognized, the rate of development is important for an underdeveloped country. Individual industrialists in India have neither the capital nor the technical resources to make adequate investment for a reasonably rapid expansion in our economy, which on the other hand cannot expand without help. The State, obviously, has to supplement. Hence the conclusion that a mixed economy is the best solution to the problem of growth. It is quite false to insinuate that our plan gives all economic initiative to the State; on the contrary, the field open to private enterprise is a wide one and it is the essence of the planned approach to harmonize the public and private sectors. The scope of the public sectors is confined to heavy and basic industries, transport and communications, power, multi-purpose projects and strategic controls, etc., whereas the production of consumer goods and the sphere of agriculture are open to private enterprise. However, when and if State control goes beyond the limits of stimulating development and stifles private enterprise, adjustments in policy may be necessary and advisable. By mixed economy we mean that a balance must be maintained between the public sector and private enterprise, between big industry and small-scale and cottage industry, that intensive employment at the village level must exist alongside the bigger schemes of industrialization.[1]

Mrs. Gandhi reiterated this philosophy in her first address on All-India Radio to the nation after assuming her high office, by saying,

"In our mixed economy, private enterprise has flourished and has received help and support from the government. We shall continue to encourage and assist it."[2]

LICENSING PROCEDURE

Foreign investors are now encouraged to apply for letters of intent for new industrial undertakings. The industrial license will, however, issue only to the Indian company formed to carry out the project. The foreign investor is required to find an Indian partner or arrange for the underwriting of a public issue of rupee capital which would comprise majority ownership. While this was always legally possible, the overwhelming majority of new industrial undertakings with foreign collaboration was initiated by Indian entrepreneurs. The encouragement of foreign enterprise to take the initiative is calculated to stimulate more foreign investment.

A new step was introduced in the licensing procedure in 1965. The Council of Scientific and Industrial Research has been brought into the licensing procedure and the approval of foreign collaboration. The government felt that foreign collaboration was being approved in too many cases when the know-how already existed in the country, resulting in a needless waste of scarce foreign exchange. Hereafter, when commercially exploited technical knowledge is available within the country, foreign collaboration will not be approved. The CSIR is considered the most appropriate organization for this determination. It will be represented on the Licensing Committee and appropriately associated with the Foreign Agreements Committee. Prospective licensees will be required to contact the CSIR and base their proposed industrial undertakings on indigenous know-how whenever available.

This new policy and procedure will raise some problems. Under many existing technical collaboration agreements, Indian companies are not free to grant the know-how to another Indian company. Many of the new companies may not have the technical manpower or training facilities for collaboration with the prospective licensee. Some may even indulge in dilatory tactics to delay or prevent the prospective competitor from acquiring the know-how and starting his enterprise. Presumably, the new licensee will be permitted to seek his collaboration abroad if he can demonstrate that the know-how is not readily available, even if existent, in the country. Un-co-operative companies, on the other hand, can be expected to be dealt with harshly, particularly if the proposed Monopolies and Restrictive Trade Practices Bill is enacted.

The Pakistan war sharpened the defense orientation of industrial development. A representative of the Defense Ministry has, therefore, been added to the Licensing Committee.

LICENSING POLICIES

Defense against China and Pakistan and the increasing shortage of foreign exchange have become the two dominant considerations in industrial licensing and foreign collaboration approval. Self-sufficiency in industry and export of manufactured goods are the main objectives in coping with the foreign exchange shortage.

As already mentioned, foreign technical collaboration will not be approved if the know-how is commercially available in India. Foreign collaborations will be required to demonstrate that they will be self-sufficient in components and raw materials within three years before obtaining approval. Exceptions shall, of course, have to be made in case of raw materials not indigenously available, such as copper and other nonferrous metals. But even in these cases the approval will not be easy to obtain. Most approvals will be conditioned on exports by the new enterprise to earn the foreign exchange for the raw materials required from outside India.

None of these are new criteria in industrial licensing policy. The foreign exchange shortage vests them with new emphasis. They will be enforced more strictly, instead of loosely, as in the past.

The Fourth Plan places the highest priority on industries pertaining to agriculture and manufactures that can be exported.[3] Foreign collaboration will, therefore, be sought most earnestly for the manufacture of chemical fertilizers and pesticides. Tractors and farm implements are given high priority, but in this field India is already relatively self-sufficient.

Machine making will continue its high priority, particularly for export purposes, but in this area also, India is approaching self-sufficiency. It will therefore be difficult to secure foreign collaboration approval for this purpose during the Fourth Plan. Most promising in this respect are components for machines that are still being imported.

Petro-chemicals and metals will enjoy high priority with great scope for foreign collaboration. Foreign collaboration will be welcome and sought in areas where the country does not yet possess the industrial know-how and skills to start new undertakings without outside help. This is best determined through the Department of Technical Development.

Exemption from industrial licensing may be expected as self-sufficiency is attained in certain industries. In May, 1966, the Ministry of Industry freed from licensing eleven industries; iron and steel castings and forgings, iron and steel structurals, electric motors less than 10 hp, pulp, power alcohol, solvent extracted oils, glue and gelatin, glass, ceramic fire bricks, cement and gypsum products, and timber products. Additional industries are under consideration for exemption from licensing.

The criteria used for selection of industries for exemption from industrial licensing were mainly indigenous self-sufficiency on components and raw materials. Small-scale and cottage industries in need of protection were not placed on the exempt list. An additional factor was the promotion of industries having export potential.

The government made clear that this initial step toward exemption from industrial licensing was experimental and its operation would be kept under close review.

ECONOMIC CONCENTRATION

The Monopolies Inquiry Commission established in April, 1964, made its report and recommendations in December, 1965. The commission was comprised of K. C. Das Gupta, chairman, G. R. Rajagopaul, K. R. P. Aiyangar, R. C. Dutt, and I. G. Patel, members. Its terms of reference were as follows:

(a) to inquire into the extent and effect of concentration of economic power in private hands and the prevalence of monopolistic and restrictive practices in important sectors of economic activity other than agriculture with special reference to—

(i) the factors responsible for such concentration and monopolistic and restrictive practices;

(ii) their social and economic consequences, and the extent to which they might work to the common detriment; and

(b) to suggest such legislative and other measures that might be considered necessary in the light of such enquiry, including, in particular, any new legislation to protect essential public interests and the procedure and agency for the enforcement of such legislation.[4]

The report contains the best survey to date of the private sector in India. The industrial field was analyzed by product and by industrial groups. The commission found economic concentration in both respects.

The criteria used for product-wise concentration was to consider it high where the share of the three top producers was 75 per cent or more; medium where it was 60 to 75 per cent; and low where it was 50 to 60 per cent. Where it was less than 50 per cent, no concentration was considered present.

In general, considerable concentration was found in the new mechanical, electrical, mineral, chemical, pharmaceutical, and related industries. A different pattern was found in the old industries. No concentration was found in jute and cotton textiles, sugar, tea, coffee, and salt.

Single producers exist in many of the new industrial items. In tools, there were thirty-four single producers in sixty-six items; seventeen out of seventy-one items in industrial machinery; twenty-two out of seventy-one products in the metallurgical industries; and so on in most of the new industrial categories.

High concentration was found in various important industrial areas. Three concerns produced motor cars with Hindustan Motors, accounting for 66.1 per cent; Standard Motor Products of India, 17.2 per cent; and Premier Automobiles, 16.7 per cent. Aluminum had three producers with Indian Aluminum in the lead with 48.2 per cent, and Hindustan Aluminum came next with 38.5 per cent of the production. The combined products of three top producers of steel pipe and tubes exceeded 75 per cent: Indian Tube Co. with 45.1 per cent; Zenith Steel Pipes with 15.7 per cent; and Kalinga Tubes with 15.8 per cent of the production.

R. C. Dutt filed a note of dissent on a number of matters. He questioned whether product-wise concentration was a matter of great concern and pointed out that in a newly industrializing country it was inevitable to have single or few producers of a new product. Moreover, it was in the best interests of rapid industrialization to permit and even encourage the new undertakings to expand in order to achieve economy of scale in production as soon as possible. Mr. Dutt felt that control of many different industries by industrial families or groups was a more serious concern.

The commission found such country-wise concentration, as it is referred to in the report, to be quite prevalent. Seventy-five groups (comprising 1,536 companies) with assets of 2605.95 crores ($56 billion), comprise approximately 46.9 per cent of the total assets of all companies in the private sector, excluding banking companies. The half dozen largest industrial groups include the following:

Group	($ million) Assets	Sales
1. Tata	808	683
2. Birla	569	609
3. Martin Burn	304	229
4. Bangur	122	137
5. Associated Cement	160	92
6. Thapar	130	149

The commission was not particularly alarmed by the concentration it found. While it deplored the social consequences of a small percentage of the population becoming very rich, which inevitably led to certain evils, such as the conspicuous flaunting of wealth and attempts to corrupt politicians and officials, it concluded that concentration promoted economic development. The report presents the following summary:

We have already indicated the view that the concentration of economic power has helped the economic betterment of the country. Even today our industrial development is far behind that in the western world or in Japan. But what little development there is owes much to the adventure and skill of a few men who have in the process, succeeded also in becoming "big business" thus concentrating in their hands a great portion of the economic power controlling and directing the production and distribution of national wealth and income. It is fair also to state that after concentrating power in their hands these men have gone on often to push forward development of further industries, which has been to the advantage of the country. It is also generally agreed that concentrated economic power has been responsible for the greater part of the not very high capital formation in the country. Huge profits were often earned so that even after the distribution of high rates of dividends good surpluses were left. These were utilized to add to the industrial capital, whether by way of issue of bonus shares or in the shape of reserves or by investment in fresh ventures.

Although complaints were not infrequently heard that dynastic control of big business has sometimes kept professional managerial talent from coming into its own, it is fair to say that big business has generally been able to supply over the years considerable amount of managerial skill of high quality, so that production has been high, profits have been good and failures comparatively few in number.

It is important to note that big business has been able to attract and obtain foreign collaboration and such collaboration has helped the starting of many industries especially by supplying the essential machinery and technical know-how. As we have already stated when discussing the factors responsible for concentration of economic power, foreign business concerns are not likely to extend similar collaboration to small units.

From its past records in the development of industries and the special advantage it has in starting and keeping up capital intensive industries and also the bright chance of obtaining helpful foreign collaboration, it is reasonable to expect that concentrated economic power may be relied upon to make an important contribution to industrial development in the crucial years to come.[5]

It is interesting to note what the commission concluded on the effect of the licensing procedure and foreign collaboration on economic concentration:

For numerous reasons, big business was at an advantage in securing licenses for starting new industries or for expanding the existing capacity. In the first place, big businessmen were in a better position to raise the large amounts of capital required for modern plants in most industries. The risk therefore of the license remaining unutilized was less in their case, than in the case of smaller businessmen. Secondly, as one leading industrialist put it "only the already successful are able to some extent to expand and proliferate; in a developing economy such as ours, success must be the principal consideration." Licensing authorities were naturally inclined to prefer men who have proved their ability by success in big industrial ventures in the past to men who had still to establish their ability.

The third reason why big businessmen succeeded in getting new licenses was their ability to secure foreign collaboration. Foreign manufacturers of goods having a good market in India or having a scope of a good market here, finding themselves handicapped by tariff measures or import restrictions lent a willing ear to requests of Indian industrialists for collaboration for manufacturing the articles on Indian soil, which would turn the restrictions to an advantage. There can be no doubt that foreign collaboration has played an important part in hastening the production in the country of many essential commodities and the quick building up of a few industries which might have otherwise taken several decades. Foreign collaboration could however be successfully wooed in the important industries only by people who already had a reputation for themselves and were believed to be financially strong. That this is so, was stated before us by several leading industrialists, and we think that this is the correct position.

We wish to make it clear that we are expressing here no opinion on the need or propriety of obtaining foreign collaboration. Indeed, a leading industrialist, who led one of the important Chambers of Commerce, was very bitter about the part foreign collaboration was playing in the industrialization of the country and the price paid for it.

Whatever be the rights and wrongs of foreign collaboration agreements, we think it to be a fact that the presence of a foreign collaborator of repute weighs with the licensing authorities, and this, as we have mentioned already, gives an edge to the big man.

It was claimed before us by some Chambers of Commerce & Industry that the licensing system helped the de-concentration, because, it was said, that the Government when issuing licenses, favoured new entrepreneurs, and smaller businessmen. Reliance was repeatedly placed in this connection on some statement that appears to have been made in Parliament in May 1963 that of 4211 licenses issued only 182 were issued to big businessmen.

To get a proper perspective of the position, we have ourselves gone through the disposal of the applications for licenses that have been refused during the five years—1959 to 1963—and have examined the reasons for such refusal. We have also compared the figures of applications for licenses made by big business and the rest, and examined how many of them were successful. After careful examination, we have come to the conclusion that there is no basis for the view that the big businessmen are at a disadvantage as compared to smaller people in the matter of obtaining licenses.

We are convinced that the system of controls in the shape of industrial licensing, however necessary from other points of view, has restricted the freedom of entry into industry and so helped to produce concentration.[6]

The commission even intimated that abolition of industrial licensing would deter economic concentration but dismissed it promptly as unfeasible at this stage of the country's economic development. It suggested instead that industrial licensing be used more positively to prevent economic concentration. In his dissenting note, Mr. Dutt said:

I am of course in complete agreement with the need to simplify licensing procedure to the maximum extent possible and to ensure that decisions are taken expeditiously, but I am unable to agree that abolition of the licensing system, even if it were possible to do so, would hold any hope of reducing or even preventing further concentration by enabling free entry into the industries of new entrepreneurs. On the other hand, I am firmly of the view that it is only by purposeful use of the licensing system that any such result can be achieved.

In regard to industrial licensing in our country, hitherto no definite policy in respect of concentration of economic power has guided the grant of licenses. Licensing has been introduced under the Industries (Development & Regulation) Act, 1948 (sic), even before the First Five Year Plan commenced. With the introduction of the Plans, it was utilized to canalise resources into industries in accordance with Plan priorities and to ensure the successful implementation of the Plan. The emphasis, however, remained on development, and this was not inconsistent as such with the Plans. An important criterion for the grant of license has accordingly been the ability of the parties seeking license to develop industrial capacity according to the Plan in the shortest possible time. This criterion has weighed in favour of established entrepreneurs and against new entrants. It is difficult to suggest that the criterion should be overlooked, for it can be ignored only at the cost of considerably slowing down the pace of development. Nevertheless, it is possible consistently with plan schedules and priorities, to take account of the factor of concentration and encourage not only promising new entrepreneurs but small established ones. It is possible, for instance, to reserve new units in conventional industries where the rate of growth envisaged by the Plan is not very high for the new entrant or the small man. For certain other industries, where the rate of planned development envisaged is higher, but which still does not enjoy a very high degree of priority, established entrepreneurs of moderate means can be encouraged. For still other industries, such as Fertilizer, Aluminum, etc. which enjoy high priorities and which are also highly capital-intensive, reliance may add to the concentration of power. I feel that if a deliberate policy of this nature is followed in the matter of licensing, the growth of the smaller man in the ancillary and low priority industries will to some extent, at any rate, compensate for the further proliferation of the larger established industrial units in the high priority capital intensive industries. I agree that a policy of this nature cannot be reduced to a set of rules or rigid principles. Each case will have to be considered on merits, but what is important is that in considering individual cases the guiding policy suggested in this paragraph should be kept firmly in mind.[7]

It may be questioned whether industrial licensing has not been used in the past to deter economic concentration. To be sure, "no definite policy" has been promulgated. At the same time, there are instances where foreign collaboration involving the big industrial groups was not approved when an acceptable alternate of smaller industrial stature was seeking the same industrial license.[8]

The commission also suggested that the public sector be used more effectively as countervailing action. Mr. Dutt re-emphasized the suggestion.

I am of the opinion that public sector should be utilized as a countervailing influence for concentration of economic power which to some extent in our present circumstances is inevitable in the private sector. I have referred earlier to the problem of dominance in industries, which cannot be prevented without loss of efficiency. Dominance in basic industries, however, does lead to concentration of economic power in private hands, and it is here that the public sector can step in to act as a countervailing force against such concentration. It must be recognized that the Industrial Policy Resolution which defines the role of the public sector has this object in view. A purposeful use of the public sector to counterbalance concentration of power in the private sector would be entirely consistent with this policy.[9]

It may be noted that to some extent this has been the case in steel, although not solely for this purpose. The private sector, that is, TISCO and IISCO, had a monopoly in steel production a decade ago. Today, the three government steel plants produce twice the steel made by the private sector plants.

Although the commission was not greatly disturbed by economic concentration *per se* (with the exception of its social and political evils) and did, in fact, conclude that economic concentration promoted industrialization of the country, it was duly concerned about its present and potential monopolistic and restrictive practices. It found that the large industrial groups made efforts to prevent competitors from establishing themselves, indulged in restrictive practices such as retail price fixation, tie-in sales, and the like. Agreements to restrict output, however, were found to be rare. Although these monopolistic practices were only nascent, their potential was disturbing. Prevention and control over such monopolistic practices were consequently made the central objective of the commission's recommendations.

The commission's recommendations comprise both policy and legislative proposals. Although the commission felt that existing powers of the government were insufficient to deal effectively with economic concentration, it nonetheless recommended:

1. that industrial licensing be used positively to prevent economic concentration,
2. that public sector enterprises be employed to countervail economic concentration, and

3. that government purchasing should be used to favor the smaller firms to increase their competitiveness.

The commission also entertained the idea that import policy be used to curb price fixing—that is, to permit or threaten to permit, imports—but ruled it out for the time being because of the foreign exchange shortage.

A difference of opinion developed between the majority and Mr. Dutt on the use of the government's power of approval over inter-corporate investments under Section 372 of the Companies Act to curb economic concentration. The majority felt this would exceed the intent of Section 372,[10] but Mr. Dutt felt that the 1963 amendments inserting the words "public interest" into the act enhanced prevention of economic concentration.[11] If such use was illegal, Mr. Dutt felt the difficulty should be surmounted by a suitable amendment.

The commission was of uncertain and divided mind on mergers and amalgamations. First, it felt it was not a present problem, as mergers and amalgamations have been rare in India to date. The commission countered:

But there is every prospect of their becoming more frequent in the future [and] in deciding what action to take about these to prevent the emergence of monopolistic conditions, we have to remember, however, that mergers and amalgamations may sometimes be called for in the best interests of the country. Horizontal mergers and amalgamations may often be an essential mode to improve efficiency and to achieve economies of scale, while vertical mergers and amalgamations may also help to cut costs. It will, in our opinion, be wrong to look upon mergers or amalgamations to be *per se* harmful to public interest. A cautious approach to the problem is therefore desirable.[12]

The majority concluded that permission for mergers and amalgamations should be sought from the permanent authority on monopolies proposed in the report. R. C. Dutt demurred on the grounds that the courts are already empowered to decide on the appropriateness of mergers and amalgamations under the Companies Act. If this legal control is not adequate, the act should be appropriately amended, he feels, instead of setting up another procedure.[13] Both thought this matter required careful consideration.

The heart of the commission's recommendation is the establishment of a permanent body to exercise vigilance and protect the country against the undesirable consequences of economic concentration.

The primary function of the body "should be directed against restrictive practices and monopolistic practices."[14]

Compulsory registration of all restrictive practices would be required by law. The publicity of the practice, it is felt, would in many cases stop such practices. This feature is borrowed from European legislation on monopolies.

The permanent body, called a "Commission" by the report, should be empowered to investigate complaints from consumers or others against restrictive practices. If the practice is found to operate to the common detriment, the commission should have power to order a discontinuation. Such orders to desist should be final and enforceable by law subject only to an appeal to the Supreme Court. Fines, but not imprisonment are prescribed as penalties for disobedience.

The "Commission" should be empowered to pass on the appropriateness of mergers and amalgamations where "dominance," defined as control over the production, supply, or distribution of one-third of a particular commodity or service, is involved. "The Commission should not give its approval . . . unless it is satisfied that its harmful effect in aggravating the monopolistic position is clearly less than its beneficial effects on the economy in the shape of higher production, lesser costs and improvement in quality."[15] Attempts at "take over" should be dealt with in the same manner.

The majority was also of the view that the commission should be empowered to pass on proposals of expansion where "dominance" was involved. Dr. I. G. Patel and R. C. Dutt dissented on grounds that all matters of expansion should be decided by the government under its industrial licensing authority.[16]

The majority view was that no curbs should be placed on countrywise concentration for it would dissuade diversification, which was considered a greater good for economic development. Mr. Dutt, however, found it difficult to agree "that no curb should be placed on diversification."

The report contains a draft bill entitled "The Monopolies and Restrictive Trade Practices Bill, 1965" incorporating the above recommendations of the commission. It is a comprehensive piece of legislation establishing and empowering a Monopolies and Restrictive Trade Practices Commission to deter concentration of economic power, to restrain monopolistic and restrictive trade practices, and providing for the registration of restrictive trade agreements, all appropriately defined and delineated.

It is noteworthy that the commission did not deem fit to prescribe powers to break up large enterprises. Such power would not appear necessary, for Indian enterprises are not large by American or European standards. With the exception of the Tatas, perhaps, the large Indian enterprises would be considered medium-sized, and only a few of them at that, by these outside standards. By starting early on prevention of economic concentration, it may never become necessary to break up large economic units in India.

FOREIGN COLLABORATION TERMS

The *Economic Times* surveys on foreign collaboration referred to earlier shed considerable light on the terms and conditions negotiated and approved by the Indian government.[17] The November, 1964, survey analyzes 173 agreements concluded by 131 large and medium-sized public companies. The information was derived from prospectuses, cooperative companies, and other sources. It is considered a dependable random sample.

As already stated, the average equity participation was 20 per cent. The survey did not analyze the consideration; that is, cash, machinery, and equipment, new or used, and/or capitalization of know-how and technical services, exchanged for the equity shares. Perhaps the raw material was insufficient for such analysis, but it can be hoped that future surveys will contain this information.

Eighty-eight of the collaboration agreements involved some equity participation. This reflects a rising foreign investment content in foreign collaboration in India, but only 30 of the agreements involved one-third or more equity participation by the foreign collaboration. Only seven agreements gave the foreign collaborator majority ownership; eight provided for 50 per cent ownership; and none exceeded 60 per cent.

Royalty provisions were found in 52 of the agreements. No uniformity was found in the royalty provisions. Most were based on gross or net sales; some on units of production; others on profits. The royalty ranged from 0.5 per cent to a high of 5 per cent found in seven cases. In the overwhelming number of agreements, the royalty ranged between 2 and 3 per cent of net sales.

It is significant that several agreements provided a royalty only for export sales or a higher rate for exports. The Corning Glass—Borosil Glass collaboration provides a royalty of 3 per cent on export sales.

The Michle–Goss–Indian Graphic Arts Equipment Co. agreement provides a 5 per cent commission on foreign sales and 3 per cent royalty on net sales. The Westinghouse–Usha Refrigeration agreement prescribes 4 per cent on internal sales and 5 per cent on exports. A few other agreements contain similar provisions.

Fees for know-how and technical services likewise reflect no uniformity. About half of the agreements provide a fee payment but less than half of them provided for a fee exceeding $100,000. Only four agreements provided a fee in excess of a million dollars.

Most revealing is the information brought forth on the over-all limitation. The thirty agreements involving one-third or more equity participation also provided for other payments with the exception of eleven cases, but only five collaborations called for both royalties and technical fees. Six provided additionally for royalties only, and nine for technical fees only. The five providing for both are worth noting in detail as they serve to give foreign enterprise a general idea of the outside parameter of the over-all limitation on collaboration terms.

The Associated Bearing–SKF collaboration involved a 60 per cent SKF equity participation plus a 2.5 per cent royalty on net sales and a $88,200 technical fee. The total project cost is estimated at $12 million.

The Chemicals & Fibres–Imperial Chemicals Industries agreement grants Imperial Chemicals 60 per cent of the equity shares, plus a 2.5 to 3.5 per cent royalty on net sales and a $560,000 technical fee. The project cost was approximately $12 million.

Elpro International agreed to grant General Electric 50 per cent of the equity, together with a 3 per cent royalty on net sales and a payment of $793,800 for supply of machinery and technical services. The size of the project was approximately $3.5 million.

The Michle–Goss–Indian Graphic Arts Equipment Co. collaboration allows the American collaborator a 50 per cent equity participation, a 3 per cent royalty on net sales, a 5 per cent commission on export sales, and a small technical fee of $31,500. The project cost was approximately $1.5 million.

Prestolite of India granted a 44 per cent equity participation to Autolite of U.S.A., a 4 per cent royalty on net sales less imported components, and a technical fee of $17,000. The project cost was approximately $1 million.

This sample of foreign collaboration terms reveals that only a small number of agreements provide for royalties and fees where the equity participation is substantial. Where they do so provide, the royalty seldom exceeds 3 per cent and the fee is small. It should also be noted that the collaborations involved important items in the industrial structure of the country, such as ball bearings, automotive components, polyester fibres, and the like.

GOVERNMENT TAKEOVER

The Industries Development Amendment Act, 1965, changed Section 18A, imposing a limit of fifteen years for a takeover of management of an industrial undertaking. Hereafter, when the initial period of five years in a takeover under Section 18A expires, the government may extend control of the industrial undertaking for any period up to a limit of ten years, but no more than ten years.

Twelve industrial units have been taken over to date. The general consensus is that these enterprises have been run efficiently by the government, thereby preventing their shutdown with consequent loss of production and employment.

Most of the takeovers involved small family textile and sugar concerns. A notable exception was Jessop & Co., Ltd., of Calcutta, a leading heavy-engineering firm of long standing. Its management was assumed by the government in the public interest in May, 1958, when it was acquired and mismanaged by Haridas Mundhra. The control has been extended from time to time under Section 18A, the last extension being effective until May, 1967.

In view of Jessop's importance to the national economy and defense, the government decided to purchase majority control from the shareholders.[18] An agreement for the purchase of 1,123,000 shares was concluded with a number of companies and individuals on August 18, 1965. The agreement provided that the question of price for the shares was to be decided by an independent arbitrator, mutually agreed on, who shall be a retired judge of the Supreme Court. The arbitrator shall determine the market price of the shares as of the date of the agreement, and the shareholders agreeing to sell to the government shall receive such market price or Rs 25 per share, whichever is less. The arbitrator's award is to be final. The closing market price of the shares on the Calcutta Exchange on August 18, 1965, was Rs 25.62.

COMMODITY CONTROLS

Nothing has generated greater controversy inside and outside India than the wisdom of continuing distribution and price control of essential commodities. Industries subject to price control allege they are being deprived of both internal and external capital for expansion. Outside organizations interested in India's development, such as the World Bank, have urged a relaxation or elimination of commodity controls as a way of generating more private investment and economic development.

It should be noted that the government has been relaxing price controls progressively the past few years as the production situation warrants. In 1963 it removed controls over sixteen important commodities,[19] and in 1965 controls on special quality steels and pig iron were lifted. The most important step, however, was the removal of controls on the price and distribution of cement, excepting quantities required by the government, in early 1966. Decontrol will encompass about 50 per cent of production sold to customers other than government.

Cement decontrol is something of an experiment. Cement is still in short supply; capacity at the end of the Third Plan was about 12.5 million tons. It is planned to double production capacity during the Fourth Plan. Decontrol is calculated to facilitate the generation of finance for this monumental expansion.

As expected, the Cement Manufacturers Association announced a price increase of Rs 16 per ton starting January 1, 1966. The association's president, G. D. Somani, stated that the cement manufacturers agreed not to use any of the increased Rs 16 crores of profits derived from the price increase for payment of dividends, devoting the entire amount, instead, to expansion. He said the industry had plans to add 10 million tons of production in the next five or six years.[20]

The association promptly set up a sales co-ordinating organization with regional offices at Delhi, Bombay, Calcutta, and Madras, to undertake the responsibility of distribution performed by the State Trading Corporation under the Cement Control Order.

Commodity control became a controversial issue in foreign collaboration for fertilizer projects. Many of the prospective collaborators urged strongly that the government permit them complete freedom to market the fertilizer; that is, set prices and develop the market.

The government has made it known that such decontrol may now be negotiated for a period of seven years after start of production, with the exception that a certain portion of the production shall be sold to the government at a negotiated price.

These recent developments bespeak, again, the basic policy of the government to resort to commodity controls, mainly price control, only insofar as is necessary to avert undesirable inflation that would undermine sound and orderly economic development. The private sector, domestic and foreign, should understand, however, that the government would have no hesitation on reimposition of controls if found necessary to protect the rupee, which has remained one of the world's soundest currencies during the post-war period.

VII

Protection of New Industries

Import control continues as the dominant policy for the protection of new Indian industries from foreign competition. Import restrictions are not, however, used solely for this purpose. In fact, their dominant purpose is the careful husbanding of scarce foreign exchange resources. In this purpose, of course, import controls provide indigenous industry freedom from foreign competition. Tariff policy, designed specifically for such purpose, remains overshadowed in the background.

It is interesting to note in the Monopolies Commission Report that there is some questioning of the absolute protection from foreign competition afforded Indian industries by import restrictions.[1] There is a feeling it deprives the economy of a disciplinary factor for promoting more efficient production and lower prices. Tariffs are considered a better protective policy as they can be handled with greater flexibility. It was felt, however, that in view of the extreme shortage of foreign exchange, the country could not afford any other policy at this time.

IMPORT DEPOSIT SCHEME

In June, 1964, the Reserve Bank announced that a deposit of 25 per cent of the value of the proposed imports would be required before sanction of foreign exchange. The purpose of the import deposit was to slow down imports. There was an immediate outcry from Indian entrepreneurs who had arranged foreign credits or investment for new projects. The Reserve Bank promptly made appropriate exemptions for six categories of imports:

1. Capital goods imported under licenses issued on approved deferred payment terms
2. Capital goods paid for out of share subscriptions made in cash

by foreign collaborators as approved by the Government of India and retained abroad with the permission of the Reserve Bank of India for the specific purpose of making payment for the goods to be imported

3. Capital goods imported against issue of shares to foreign collaborators as approved by the government of India and the Reserve Bank of India

4. Goods imported under licenses stipulating payment out of foreign governments, foreign collaborators, foreign or Indian institutions, or any other persons and paid for by the letter of committment procedure, or by any other procedure approved by the Reserve Bank and providing in either case for direct payment to the supplier from out of the proceeds of such foreign exchange loans

5. Cotton, cotton seed oil, soya bean oil, and mutton tallow imported and paid for under PL 480 arrangements

6. Any goods for which an import license is not required

The deposit requirement applied to imports by the government and its companies or agencies, such as the State Trading Corporation. The scheme was considered temporary. It was terminated in June, 1966.

Import duties were also increased in 1965 to dissuade imports. Further similar restrictions on imports can be expected for a number of years until India achieves a more favorable balance of trade.

EXPORT PROMOTION

The main effort toward a favorable balance of trade is a vigorous export drive. The past few years have seen an augmentation of the export promotion schemes. The Fourth Plan aims at 5,100 crores of exports. This, every Indian realizes, is going to take some doing.

Export promotion has been elevated in status. A separate ministry, first named the Ministry of International Trade, now called the Ministry of Commerce, was constituted for the purpose. It is headed by an energetic young man, Manubhai Shah and was elevated to cabinet rank in the new Gandhi administration.

In addition to general promotional work and assistance to Indian manufacturers and traders, the government instituted three basic programs to facilitate exports. They were:

1. Import entitlements for raw materials, components, and other industrial requirements

2. Tax concessions
3. Export credits and guarantees

The greatest obstacle, perhaps, to increasing exports is the high price of Indian manufactured goods. It might be noted at this point that the export of manufactured goods is the main hope of increased export earnings as the country achieves industrialization. The recent trends in India's exports are seen in the following tables.

The main reason for the high price of Indian manufactures is the absence, at this stage of the country's industrialization, of economy of scale in production. In due time this can be expected to be overcome. In addition, however, as the Mudalier Committee found,[2] many of these small scale units are unable to utilize their full capacity because of insufficient raw materials or components that must be imported.

In order to alleviate this problem, the government first started to issue import entitlements to exporters. These entitlements were usually based on past exports, but some were issued against anticipated exports. The basic tenet underlying the scheme was to entitle an exporter to a quota of his export earnings for imports of raw materials or components he needed in his manufacture. These quotas were based upon the import component of the exports and the export priority assigned to the particular product. The quotas and related matters were worked out by Export Promotion Councils consisting of business representatives and officials. Others, such as the Coir Board and textile commissioner were assigned the task for certain schemes. There are some twenty-three export promotion schemes now in being.[3] The functions of the councils are described in the Handbook of Export Promotion in the following brief:

EXPORTS STRUCTURE OF INDIA
(EXPORTS)

(Rs. in lakhs)

Category	1960-61	1961-62	1962-63	1963-64	1964-65	% change in '64-65 over 1960-61
1	2	3	4	5	6	7
1. Food	19805	21402	23395	24987	26066	31.6
2. Beverages & tobacco	1577	1499	1888	2252	2591	64.3
3. Crude materials, in-edible except fuels	11206	11833	11108	13198	13946	24.5

Category	1960-61	1961-62	1962-63	1963-64	1964-65	% change in '64-65 over 1960-61
1	2	·3	4	5	6	7
4. Minerals fuels, lubricants & related materials	741	590	648	976	1273	71.8
5. Animal and vegetable oils and fats	980	649	1365	2060	742	—24.3
6. Chemicals	719	783	784	690	986	37.7
7. Manufactured goods	26334	26978	26669	31948	34883	32.5
8. Machinery and transport equipment	719	474	647	706	930	29.3
Total exports	64232	66034	68548	79324	83870	30.6

DIRECTION OF INDIA'S FOREIGN TRADE

(Rs. in lakhs)

1	1960-61	1961-62	1962-63	1963-64	1964-65	% change in '64-65 over 1960-61
	2	3	4	5	6	7
All countries	64232	66034	68548	79324	83870	30.6
Western Hemisphere	13826	14998	15668	17182	18605	34.6
U.S.A.	10253	11574	11433	12989	15110	47.4
Western Europe	23985	22887	23471	25115	24569	2.4
E.E.C. Countries	5175	5182	4882	6219	5774	
Eastern Europe	4956	6379	9236	10891	14843	199.5
U.S.S.R.	2881	3220	3825	5210	8242	
Other E. E. Countries	2075	3159	5412	5681	6601	
Middle East	5299	5455	5321	5608	5596	5.6
Other Africa	2338	2995	2540	2366	2438	4.3
Other Asia (Excluding U.S.S.R.)	10757	10886	9709	15547	15061	40.0
South East	3552	3156	2920	4559	4687	
Far East	7205	7730	6789	10987	10373	
Oceania	3071	2434	2602	2615	2758	

They guide new-comers to the export trade by giving advice on different markets, furnishing the names of importers in those markets, and informing them of shipping procedure, etc. They undertake market studies and furnish the results thereof to the trade. They also facilitate contact between the Indian exporters and foreign importers by publishing directories and other literature pertaining to industry and trade. Their other publications include market survey reports, bulletins, etc. They conduct propaganda through exhibitions, showrooms, bulletins and other media of publicity. They secure samples from foreign markets of similar goods competing with Indian goods preferred by foreign consumers and exhibit them to manufacturers in the country so as to enable them to produce goods of similar variety for export. They administer export promotion schemes and render assistance to exporters in obtaining controlled indigenous materials, priority in rail transport and other similar facilities. They administer quality control schemes, e.g., cashew and spices, and persuade Indian exporters and foreign buyers to avail themselves of the facilities in regard to quality control. They help in the amicable settlement of commercial disputes, and help the trade in drawing up a code of conduct and standard contract forms. When there is a dispute between Indian exporters and foreign importers of Indian goods, the Councils depute their overseas officers to witness the survey of goods exported from India.[4]

One of the most important was the Special Export Promotion Scheme for Engineering Goods, headed by the Engineering Export Promotion Council with headquarters in Calcutta. The council has regional offices in London, Dusseldorf, Singapore, Beirut, and Mombasa.

This scheme set up a subcommittee of the council to administer it. The joint chief controller of imports and exports, Calcutta, and the iron and steel controller or their nominees were members of the subcommittee. Exporters, whether manufacturers or traders, were required to register if they wished to benefit in the scheme. Both old and new exporters were eligible.

The subcommittee investigated the background, reputation, and experience of the applicant before registration. Once registered, the exporter remained listed unless an interval of eighteen months elapsed without an application for an import entitlement, the exporter violated the conditions of registration, or indulged in some corrupt or fraudulent practice. Such exporter was given an opportunity to offer an explanation before being registered.

The benefits granted a registered exporter under the scheme were:

1. Import entitlements, as listed in Annexure V to the scheme

2. Allocation and supply of indigenous raw materials and other industrial requirements

The import entitlements were fixed by the Ministry of Commerce in consultation with the council, based on information regarding the quantities of different materials, imported and indigenous, used in the manufacture of the export and the CIF value of the imported materials. The import entitlements varied considerably. For example, the export of electric motors had a 40 per cent import entitlement, diesel engines 75 per cent, and copper, brass, and aluminum products 100 per cent. The reason for the latter was that India is almost completely dependent on imports of nonferrous metals. The quotas were based on the FOB value of the exports.

In general, import entitlements were allowed to registered exporters on production of proof of export and/or receipt of the payment for export. The entitlement was usually based on the preceding monthly, quarterly, semi-annual, or annual exports. On special application, the entitlement could be requested immediately upon effecting the export.

The import entitlement could be used to import the materials listed in Annexure VII. Special application had to be made for materials not listed, with proof they are required for the manufacture of the export item. This was forwarded by the council to the Department of Technical Development for decision. Imports of machinery, including parts and testing equipment, was also allowed, with the approval of the department and where the proposed import exceeded 5 lakhs with the additional approval of the Capital Goods Committee.

The materials imported under the import entitlement could be

1. Used in the exporter's own production
2. Sold to any other manufacturer producing items covered by the scheme who exports, directly or indirectly, part of his production

The exporter could also transfer or sell his import entitlement, or import license thereunder, to such manufacturer. Details of such sales or transfers to others had to be reported to the council within a fortnight.

There was no restriction on selling the import entitlement at a premium; sometimes these ran as high as 50 per cent. The premium was a matter of negotiation between buyer and seller and was viewed as a device for enabling the exporter to cut his export price and recoup the loss in whole or in part through a premium sale of his import entitlement. There were obvious limitations on the practice, as the exporter could only afford to transfer the import entitlement in excess of his own needs. But some of the entitlements proved to be quite liberal, doubtless with this export promotional intent in mind.

Import licenses under the scheme were normally issued against exports already made. Advance licenses could, however, be issued where a firm order for export had been secured by the applicant. Advance licenses were not issued for import of machinery and parts.

The import entitlements were not allowed for exports to Nepal, Tibet, Sikkim, Bhutan, and Afghanistan. Exports under rupee trade agreements were granted import entitlements only for imports from such rupee payment countries.

The council was responsible for checking up on the use of the import entitlements and the materials imported thereunder to assure that the exporters were conforming to the scheme. Progress reports had to be made to the Ministry of Commerce quarterly with copies to the deputy chief controller of export promotion in Calcutta.

Various tax concessions were also accorded exports, and export duties had been reduced and abolished in most cases. Import duties paid on imported materials used in the production of the exports are refunded, as are excise duties on indigenous materials. Exporters are also permitted to manufacture in bond under Section 65 of the Customs Act and Rule 19B of the Central Excise Rules, thereby avoiding payment of import or excise duties on the materials used for the production of export items.

Rebates on income tax and tax credit certificates for exports were authorized by the Finance Acts of 1964 and 1965. These income tax concessions will be discussed in detail in Chapter XI.

After devaluation of the rupee in June, 1966, the import entitlement and tax concession schemes were abolished in favor of a new approach to export promotion. First, maintenance imports, that is, raw materials and components, were freed of import restrictions with respect to fifty-nine categories of industries. Second, outright monetary subsidies, ranging from 10 to 20 per cent of the FOB value, were granted for the export of certain goods like engineering goods, metal scrap, iron and steel, woolen carpets, sugar, and others. Both are designed to give the same incentives and advantages as the old schemes but in a greatly simplified manner.

Export credit facilities also have been established. Export finance is provided, mainly, by commercial banks including the State Bank of India. The Reserve Bank and Refinance Corporation for Industry refinance such credits. The State Trading Corporation also provides some export finance, but the most important is the Export Credit and Guarantee Corporation that assumes various commercial and political risks involved in export credit and finance.

To suit the varying needs of the exporters, the ECGC provides different types of covers, which may be divided into the following three broad groups:

1. Standard policies issued to exporters to protect them against the risks of trading with overseas buyers on credit terms
2. Financial guarantees issued to banks against the risks involved in providing credit to exporters
3. Special policies

Under its policies intended to protect the exporters against overseas credit risks, the ECGC bears the main brunt of the risk and pays the exporter 80 per cent of his loss on account of "commercial" risks and 85 per cent of the loss in the case of "political" risks.

The "commercial" risks covered are:

1. The insolvency of the buyer
2. The buyer's protracted default to pay for the goods accepted by him
3. The buyer's failure to accept the goods, when such nonacceptance is not because of the exporter's action

The "political" risks covered are:

1. Restriction on remittances in the buyer's country or any government action that may block or delay payment in rupees to the exporter
2. War, revolution, or civil disturbances in the buyer's country
3. New import licensing restrictions or cancellation of a valid import license in the buyer's country
4. Cancellation of export license or imposition of new export licensing restrictions in India
5. Additional handling, transport, or insurance charges as a result of the interruption or diversion of a voyage which cannot be recovered from the buyer
6. Any other cause of loss accruing outside India, not normally insured by commercial insurers and beyond the control of the exporter or the buyer

The ECGC does not, however, cover risks of loss because of

1. Disputes on quality
2. Causes inherent in the nature of goods
3. A buyer's failure to obtain import or exchange authorization from the appropriate authority
4. Default of an exporter or his agent
5. Fluctuations in exchange rates

An exporter may either take a comprehensive risks policy covering both political and commercial risks, or he may secure himself against political risks alone. In either case, he can secure cover from the date of shipment.

In the sphere of financial guarantees, the ECGC undertakes to share the risks of the exporter with the lending bank. The beneficiaries under the guarantees given by the ECGC are not the banks alone but the exporters as well. These guarantees have been designed to assist and encourage banks to give liberal credit—both pre-shipment and post-shipment for producing, packing, and exporting goods.

Three guarantees have been evolved:

1. Packing credit guarantee
2. Post-shipment credit guarantee
3. Export finance guarantee

These guarantees cover the risk of nonpayment by an exporter arising from his insolvency or default. The ECGC pays the bank 66.66 per cent of the loss in the case of the packing credit and post-shipment credit guarantee, and 75 per cent of the loss in the case of the export finance guarantee.

The ECGC has also evolved a scheme under which foreign exchange credit is made available on a revolving basis to manufacturers for import of essential raw materials destined for the export market.

VIII

Foreign Exchange Control

The Foreign Exchange Regulation Act was amended in December, 1964, mainly to strengthen the enforcement machinery and to correct certain deficiencies in the scheme of exchange control. Smuggling of foreign exchange appears to have reached disturbing proportions under the loose enforcement powers and procedures of the 1947 act. For instance, remittances of Indian settlers in Singapore fell from Rs 18.9 crores in 1956-57 to Rs 3.1 crores in 1961-62.[1]

The customs, excise, and police officers were empowered to assist the enforcement officers, as were all central and state government officers employed in any port or airport and any other officer specified by the central government by notification in the Official Gazette.[2]

The government was empowered to call for information, to search suspected persons, stop and search conveyances, search premises, examine persons, summon persons to give evidence and produce documents, and inspect books and accounts of authorized dealers.[3] Moreover, the 1964 amendments provide "if any person is found or proved to have been in possession of any foreign exchange exceeding in value two hundred and fifty rupees, the burden of proving that the foreign exchange came into his possession lawfully shall be on him."[4] Finally, the government was authorized to publish "the names and other particulars of persons who have been found guilty of any contravention of the provisions" of the act.[5]

The 1964 act singled out a few additional transactions involving foreign exchange for prior Reserve Bank approval.

The receipt, otherwise than through an authorized dealer, of any payment by order or on behalf of any person resident outside India requires general or special approval by the Reserve Bank.[6] This enables the government to prosecute recipients of illegal foreign exchange remittances.

The transfer of shares from a register outside India to a register in India needs Reserve Bank approval.[7]

The settlement of property in favor of a nonresident by will or deed of gift must now have prior Reserve Bank approval.[8] Otherwise, the settlement is void.

A person resident in India shall not give a guarantee of any debt or obligation or liability of a person resident outside India except with the general or special permission of the central government or Reserve Bank.[9]

The most important new provision affecting foreign enterprise is Section 18A. It may, therefore, be quoted in full text:

. . . a company (other than a banking company) which is not incorporated under any law in force in India or which is controlled directly or indirectly by persons resident outside India, or any branch or office of any such company in India, or a firm consisting wholly or in part of persons resident outside India, shall not accept appointment as—

(a) agent in India of any person, company or firm in the trading or commercial transactions thereof, or
(b) technical or management adviser in India of any person, company or firm,

except with the general or special permission of the Central Government or the Reserve Bank; and where such appointment is accepted without such permission, it shall be void.

Foreign corporations entering into such "service" contracts or arrangements required prior Reserve Bank approval. Indian companies controlled by foreign residents have now been placed on the same footing.

No airline, shipping company, or travel agent may book passage for any person for a journey, the whole or any part of which is, outside India, except with the general or special permission of the Reserve Bank and subject to such conditions, if any, as may be specified therein.[10]

EXCHANGE CONTROL MANUAL

The fifth edition of the *Exchange Control Manual* was published by the Reserve Bank in May, 1965, to take into account the changes made by the 1964 act and other amendments in the regulations and orders under the act. Unlike previous editions of the manual, the present edition is available for sale to the public through authorized dealers.

In general, the new manual is a refinement of its predecessor. Some of the new provisions are noteworthy.

A new section IX grants general permission to authorized dealers to furnish export guarantees. Deferred payment guarantees for imports of machinery and heavy equipment, however, require specific prior approval.

A new provision on technical collaboration payments reads as follows:

> Proposals for foreign collaboration involving payment of royalties (other than on books) or technical consultancy fees should be referred by firms and companies direct to the Ministry of the Government of India dealing with the particular industry. If the proposed arrangement is approved, the Government of India will inform the applicant of their decision, while a formal authorization under the Foreign Exchange Regulation Act will be issued by the Reserve Bank. Remittances falling due under the arrangement will, however, be subject to the prior approval of the Reserve Bank, and such applications should, therefore, be referred to the Bank, citing reference to the authorization issued by it and furnishing the particulars and documents specified in the authorization.[11]

As for the engagement of foreign nationals,

"Prior sanction of the Reserve Bank must be obtained for the engagement by residents of foreign nationals to work in India and applications should be made by letter (in duplicate) giving full particulars of the work for which such employees are required, the reasons for selecting them, the terms on which the appointment is to be made and details of the visa obtained (where necessary) for the foreigner's stay in India."[12]

Regarding payment in rupees of a foreign technician's passage to India, it is now provided, "In the case of foreign technicians whose services are engaged by a firm or a company in India, the firm or company concerned will be permitted to book the passage of the technician against payment of the fare in rupees by it if the terms of the engagement provide for this liability to be borne by it, provided the technician has been granted a business visa, where necessary, for his stay in India. While submitting such applications, therefore, documentary evidence showing grant of a business visa and a certified copy of the contract of engagement should be produced."[13]

The following provision is found in the new manual on foreign equity participation:

Applications for permission to issue shares to foreign collaborators in industrial ventures in India should be addressed direct to that Ministry of the Government of India which is concerned with the particular industry (such as the Ministry of Petroleum and Chemicals in the case of the chemical industry), irrespective of whether the foreign investment is for the establishment of new industrial units or for expansion of existing units. This procedure should be followed whether the foreign capital subscription is against an initial issue of capital to non-residents in a new company or against additional issue of capital by an existing company, even if a part or whole of its shares are already held by non-residents. The Government will inform the applicants of their decision on the application, and after it is approved by Government, the Reserve Bank will issue a formal authorization under the Foreign Exchange Regulation Act, 1947.[14]

The import and export of Indian rupees is now completely prohibited except with the general or special permission of the Reserve Bank. Before February, 1963, a person could bring in or take out up to Rs 75 without permission.

In sum, the control of foreign exchange has been tightened considerably and the enforcement provisions greatly strengthened the past few years. This will doubtless make more difficult the illegal exchanges of Indian rupees for foreign currencies.

INDIAN COLLABORATION ABROAD

Pursuant to government encouragement and Reserve Bank approval, Indian companies are entering into industrial collaborations abroad involving both equity participation and technical collaboration. A number of collaborations have been entered into by Indian companies in the Middle East and Africa. This effort is part of the country's export drive to ease the foreign exchange shortage.

Somewhat unusual and most interesting in this respect is the government's approval of the purchase of a controlling interest in F. H. Schule, Gmbh. of Hamburg, Germany, which manufactures agricultural processing and other machinery, by Kirloskar Oil Engines, Ltd. Acquisition of control of the German firm by Kirloskar will enable it to develop its exports to Germany and Europe. Furthermore, it will derive technical assistance from its German subsidiary for the manufacture in India of a wide range of agricultural machinery and equipment.

The Reserve Bank gave Kirloskar permission to purchase 75 per cent of the shares from the Schule family for Rs 62 lakhs ($1.3 million), one half to be paid immediately and one half in five equal half-yearly installments. Kirloskar was authorized to pay 40 lakhs in DMs from a loan extended it by the Bank of Baroda, with the balance of 22 lakhs to be paid out of its export earnings through the German subsidiary. The Bank of Baroda loan is repayable over an eight-year period with interest at 9 per cent per annum.

Foreign collaboration appears to be developing into a two-way street. This promises to give a new dimension to foreign enterprise in India.

DEVALUATION OF THE RUPEE

The rupee was devalued to Rs 7.5 to the dollar and Rs 21 to the pound sterling on June 6, 1966. The primary reason stated by the government for the devaluation was to provide a powerful stimulant to exporters and increase the foreign exchange earnings of the country. The increased export earnings should also afford exporters greater leeway for competitive pricing of Indian goods in the world markets. The government, however, retained some degree of control over this aspect through export duties on the leading export items.

As already noted, devaluation was followed by a reformation of import controls and the export promotion schemes. Maintenance imports for fifty-nine industries were freed of import controls. This change was aimed at bringing idle industrial capacity into full production. The new monetary export subsidies were established to simplify export promotion. At first, it was thought that devaluation *ipso facto* would encourage greater exports, but later it was concluded that some form of export subsidies would have to be continued.

The devaluation proved controversial inside India. Indian opinion was sharply divided on its necessity and benefits. The economics of devaluation remains unconvincing to many. There had been deterioration in the value of the rupee but not as much as in the currencies of many other countries. The rise in the wholesale price index since 1953 was about 75 per cent, most of which took place the past three years, largely because of food shortages. There was only a 2.8 per cent increase per year during the decade preceding the recent rise. The prevailing conviction in India is that the devaluation was the price paid for continued foreign aid from the consortium of western countries and institutions. At the moment, both the increased foreign aid and the beneficial results of devaluation are slow in coming, leading to further misgivings about the devaluation inside India. The step is, however, irrevocable.

Devaluation also disturbed economic relations with the Soviet bloc countries, many of which had rupee trade agreements with India. The Government of India took immediate steps to renegotiate these agreements on the basis of the new value of the rupee. The results were favorable, as Russia and some other bloc countries were willing to absorb most of the losses involved.

Foreign investment, likewise, suffered losses because of the devaluation. Foreign investments declined 36.5 per cent in value. Equity investments can be expected to overcome the loss in value over the long run. Loans and debentures, unless the principal amount is stated in dollars, suffer the full 36.5 per cent loss in value. Where the foreign loan is stated in dollars the repayments burden of the Indian company in rupees increased by 67.5 per cent—a further detriment to any foreign equity investment in such Indian company. Dividends and royalties will be similarly discounted. Some of this loss may be made up if devaluation enables the Indian company to increase its production and profits.

In general, foreign investment made before devaluation suffered appreciable loss because of the devaluation of the rupee. On the other hand, prospective foreign investment will obtain a better share of the equity participation in Indian companies for the same dollar of cash, machinery, equipment, or know-how brought to India. This has created problems for foreign collaborations that were in mid-stream at the time of devaluation, because the negotiated equity relations were changed in favor of the foreign collaborator. In some cases the same amount of foreign investment resulted in majority ownership. New accommodations had to be worked out between the partners, which in turn necessitated reapproval of the government.

IX

Business Organization

There have been three major amendments to the Companies Act, 1956, to date. The most comprehensive, the Companies (Amendment) Act, 1960, was designed to complete company law reform begun shortly after independence and to eliminate some of the oversights and inconsistencies found in the 1956 act after it went into operation. The 1963 and 1965 amending acts were largely the outgrowth of the Bose report on the Dalmia-Jain companies.[1] The report resulted from the inquiry of a commission, headed by retired Justice Vivian Bose, into the corporate malpractices of the Dalmia-Jain industrial group. The government subsequently requested that Attorney-General C. K. Dapthary and retired Justice A. V. Viavanatha Sastri examine the report and recommendations of the Bose Commission and make suggestions for amending the act.[2]

To recapitulate, the Companies (Amendment) Act, 1963, passed by Parliament in December, 1963, and effective from January 1, 1964, made the following important changes and additions:

1. The constitution of a tribunal, redesignated "Companies Tribunal" by the 1965 act, for decision of cases referred to it of fraud or serious irregularities in the management of companies, with powers to remove persons found guilty and the transfer to the tribunal of all or any of the powers conferred on the court under Sections 155, 203, 240 and 397-407, which the central government may specify

2. The constitution of the Company Law Board in place of the original Company Law Administration

3. The appointment of a public trustee for the exercise of voting rights of shares held in trust

4. The empowering of the central government to convert govern-

ment loans to companies into shares in that company without having to obtain its approval in a general meeting

5. The authorization of companies to issue convertible debentures to certain specified institutions without the need of a special resolution

6. The enlargement of the scope of Sections 397, 398, 408 to include the public interest

In sum, the procedures and powers of the government were enlarged to intervene in company affairs to prevent corporate malpractices and inadequacies and to protect the public interest. A significant step taken by the government pursuant thereto will be discussed subsequently.

The new tribunal was constituted with B. N. Gokhale, retired judge of the Maharasthra High Court, as chairman, and G. Mathias of the Indian Audit and Accounts Service, as member. M. N. Kaul, a former Lok Sabha secretary, was appointed public trustee with powers to vote shares held in trust pursuant to Section 187B of the act.

In 1964, a new Section 635B was enacted, first by ordinance, later replaced by the Companies (Amendment) Act, 1964, to protect employees against victimization by company management during the course of investigation of the affairs of a company, inquiry into its true ownership and other matters, or during the pending of proceedings before the Companies Tribunal. The new section provides that when a company, during the course of such proceedings, proposes to discharge or punish an employee, it must so intimate in writing to the Company Law Board. If the board raises no objection within thirty days, the company may proceed with the proposed action. If the board objects, the company may, if it wishes, appeal to the tribunal within thirty days. The tribunal's decision shall be final and binding.

The Companies (Amendment) Act, 1965, enacted September 25, 1965, with effect on October 15, 1965, was designated broadly to accomplish the following:

1. Complete the reforms suggested by the Bose and Dapthary-Sastri Committee reports on corporate morality

2. Grant relief from and relax some of the procedural requirements that have proved burdensome on companies

3. Remove further inconsistencies found in the act

The significant specific changes will be noted in their respective place in the discussion hereafter.

ADMINISTRATION

The 1963 act provided for the establishment of the Company Law Board to replace the Department of Company Law Administration. Most of the powers and functions of the central government under the act were delegated to the new board on February 1, 1964.[3] Before this change in October, 1964, the old department was transferred to the Ministry of Finance, merged with the Department of Revenue, and subsequently was renamed the Department of Revenue and Company Law. In May, 1964, several additional functions, namely the administration of the Securities Contracts (Regulation) Act, 1956, the regulation of the Stock Exchanges, the Life Insurance Corporation, the Insurance Act, the Chartered Accountants Act, and others, were transferred to the department and it was renamed the Department of Company Affairs and Insurance. The Company Law Board functions under the department, and both are headed by the same official. The Department of Company Affairs was again shifted in the new cabinet set up in February, 1966, to the Ministry of Law.

PRIVATE-PUBLIC COMPANIES

The 1965 act provides that the central government may, pursuant to application, exempt an Indian private company that is owned by a foreign corporation or corporations (that, if incorporated in India, would be a private company or companies) from the application of Section 43A. Such a private company would otherwise be treated as a public company. The purpose of this amendment was to facilitate collaboration between small Indian and foreign companies.

MEMORANDUM

The 1965 act amended Section 13(c) requiring new incorporations to state separately the "main" and "other" objects of the company. The main objects are to include also "objects incidental or ancillary to the attainment of the main objects."

SHARES AND SHAREHOLDERS

Section 111 was amended by the 1965 act requiring a shareholder to appeal to the Companies Tribunal instead of the central government against any refusal of a public company or subsidiary of a public company to register a transfer of shares or debentures.

DIVIDEND DISTRIBUTION

The Department of Company Affairs ruled that it would be necessary under Section 205(2) (b) to calculate the rate of depreciation on a three-shift basis where machinery and equipment works three shifts.[4] This action was taken after the CBR allowed a third-shift allowance under the Income Tax Act in 1964.[5]

ACCOUNTS AND AUDIT

The 1965 act tightened requirements on accounts and audit. A new provision was introduced prescribing, in effect, cost accounting for certain companies.[6]

Another amendment prescribes that all relevant vouchers to any entry in the books of account shall be retained with such books for a period of eight years.[7]

In addition to being available for inspection by any director during business hours, the books of accounts must be so available to the registrar and any officer of the government authorized by the central government for this purpose. Such inspection may be made without giving any previous notice to the company. The registrar or official is empowered to make copies of or place any mark of identification on the books of account in token of the inspection.[8]

The penalty provisions for willful infraction of these provisions were extended to "all officers and other employees and agents . . . excluding bankers, auditors and legal advisors" in addition to management.[9]

The scope of audit was considerably broadened by the 1965 amendments. It is now provided that the auditor will inquire:

(a) whether loans and advances made by the company on the basis of security have been properly secured and whether the terms on which they have been made are not prejudicial to the interests of the company or its members;

(b) whether transactions of the company which are represented merely by book entries are not prejudicial to the interests of the company;

(c) where the company is not an investment company within the meaning of section 372 or a banking company, whether so much of the assets of the company as consist of shares, debentures and other securities have been sold at a price less than that at which they were purchased by the company;

(d) whether loans and advances made by the company have been shown as deposits;

(e) whether personal expenses have been charged to revenue accounts;

(f) where it is stated in the books and papers of the company that any shares have been allotted for cash, whether cash has actually been received in respect of such allotment, and if no cash has actually been so received, whether the position as stated in the account books and the balance-sheet is correct, regular and not misleading.[10]

In addition, the central government may, by general or special order, direct that, in the case of companies specified therein, the auditor's report must include a statement on such matters as it specifies in the order. The amendment prescribes that before making any such order, the government shall consult the Institute of Chartered Accountants of India about the order "unless the Government decides that such consultation is not necessary or expedient in the circumstances of the case."[11]

Finally, the central government is empowered to direct a special audit of cost accounts, additional to the regular company audit, by a cost accountant or similarly qualified person if it deems it necessary to determine if the company is complying with the new requirements on cost accounts.[12]

The new requirements are calculated to improve company accounting and prevent irregularities with company funds such as were found by the Bose Commission. Foreign enterprise should derive further comfort in the minority equity position in which it usually finds itself in a collaboration in India as a result of these new developments in company law.

It should be noted that the government has been taking various steps to improve company accounting and audit. A special committee was set up by the Council of the Institute of Chartered Accountants, at the instance of the government, to review the system and training of accountants. The council, at the suggestion of the Dapthary-Sastri Committee, formulated and published a code of conduct for chartered accountants. The institute has also published a "Statement on Auditing Practices." The Institute of Cost and Works Accountants has been doing similar work to improve the work and standards of its members.

These developments will be welcomed by foreign collaborators because the two chief difficulties in establishing new industrial undertakings in India have been production management and financial control. The government has been less than co-operative in permitting the collaborators to bring foreign cost accountants to India. Such foreign personnel are unable, for instance, to obtain tax exemption for more than six months.

DIRECTORS

The 1965 act relaxed some of the provisions on directors. No approval of the central government is required to increase the number of directors up to a maximum of twelve.[13] Reappointed directors, additional or alternate directors, those filling casual vacancies, and those named in the articles are now exempt from filing their consent in writing within thirty days of appointment with the registrar.[14] The declaration of share qualification has been omitted. The sixty-five-year age limitation provision has been repealed.

The requirement of a special resolution to sanction a director or his relative to hold any office or place of profit has been relaxed somewhat. Such resolution may now be passed in the case of the director "at a general meeting of the company held for the first time after the holding of such office or place of profit" and in the case of the relative either at such "general meeting aforesaid or within three months from the date of the appointment, whichever is later."[15]

MANAGEMENT

The restrictions on management and managerial remuneration continue to pose difficult problems. In the administration of these provisions, the department and board have stated that their objectives are "that the management of public companies does not fall into undesirable and inefficient hands and that the cost of management does not become unreasonably burdensome to the company, or manifestly in conflict with the socio-economic policies of Government."[16] But as a result of the relative severity of the restrictions, Indian entrepreneurs resort to great ingenuity to mitigate their impact.

The technical director or advisor is subjected to close scrutiny. The *Seventh Annual Report* states,

A large number of cases continued to come to the notice of the Department where Directors had been appointed as "Technical Advisors," sometimes on very high remuneration. It was contended by the companies that since technical advice was given in a capacity other than that of a director, a special resolution under Section 314 of the Act was not required for their appointment and the remuneration paid to them was outside the limits laid down for total managerial remuneration. All such cases were closely examined against the background of the management pattern of the company in the past, the technical qualifications of the persons concerned, their powers and duties, and whether such persons were rendering any managerial services to other concerns also. In most of the cases it was found that in fact the persons concerned were performing managerial services. The companies were, therefore, advised by the Department to get their appointments and remuneration regularised in the manner laid down in the Act. In almost all cases the suggestions of the Department were accepted by the companies concerned.[17]

Requests for appointment as secretaries and treasurers by former managing agents has caused concern to the department. The problem is summed up in the following words:

Mention was made in the earlier reports of Managing Agency Houses seeking their appointment as Secretaries and Treasurers in respect of some of the companies of which they were formerly acting as Managing Agents, to escape the restrictive provisions of Section 332 of the Act. During the year under review, it was observed that some of the big Managing Agency Houses which were already managing more than ten companies as Managing Agents/Secretaries and Treasurers sought appointment as Secretaries & Treasurers in some newly floated companies. In this connection, the Advisory Commission observed that in actual practice there was hardly any distinction between the functions of Managing Agents and Secretaries & Treasurers and advised that it would be desirable to impose restrictions also on the number of companies which a firm or body corporate acting as Managing Agents/Secretaries & Treasurers could manage in either capacity. The Department is keeping a watch on this tendency.[18]

And in the *Ninth Annual Report,* the department ruefully complains, "During the year, out of 1365 new companies only 6 applied for appointment of Secretaries & Treasurers to manage their affairs. Of these, in four cases, organizations which were already acting as managing agents were proposed to be appointed as Secretaries & Treasurers. Hardly a case came up where a body of professional managers was proposed for appointment."[19]

A vexing problem involves the appointment of senior executives or managers to perform various managerial services, particularly where managing agents are involved, in the management of the company. The full discussion of the problem found in the *Seventh Annual Report* is worth noting:

In paragraph 113 of the Sixth Annual Report a reference was made to the problem posed by the increasing tendency shown by the managing agents for delegation of management functions properly within the direct responsibilities of managing agents to the officers of the managed companies. The difficulties of finding a satisfactory solution to this question, in the absence of any practical formula for determining the types of functions covered by the phrase "comprehensive services" which a managing agent is expected to render to the managed company, were pointed out. This matter engaged the serious attention of the Department during the year under report and the study undertaken by its Research and Statistics Division on the basis of replies to a questionnaire issued to a representative cross-section of managing agency houses in the country was completed.

The study revealed that the nature of services rendered by managing agents to companies managed by them varied very widely. While some managing agents provided guidance on policy matters and the benefit of common expert services to their managed companies by employing whole-time paid directors and senior technical personnel, others gave only the benefit of their personal advice and guidance to the managed companies. In some cases the cost of the common expert services was borne by the managing agents while in others the entire cost of the services was distributed equitably over companies benefiting from them. The study also disclosed that it was difficult to find any reasonable common measure of services rendered by all or most of the managing agency houses in India. The Department also felt that it was not easy to distinguish between purely managerial and executive services. In the light of the results of the study, the Department came to the conclusion that by and large, an illustrative list of services which could ordinarily be regarded as falling within the scope of the direct responsibilities of the managing agents would include (a) overall supervision and control of the various operations subject to the general policy laid down by the Board of the managed company, (b) coordination and integration of information, (c) advice and guidance regarding sale of the company's products, (d) undertaking of research, (e) purchase of raw materials, import of capital goods and replacements, etc., (f) selection, training and placement of personnel, (g) planning and development, etc.

In the Department's view in respect to all these services, where senior executives or managers are employed to whom any of their powers, rights or functions are sub-delegated by the Managing Agents by a power of attorney or otherwise, the remuneration of such personnel should be paid by the Managing Agents out of the commission received by them.

Apart from the services enumerated above, the managing agents are also expected to render promotional and financial services and to maintain a central organization for providing legal, accounting, taxation, technical, secretarial and other such administrative and routine services. The expenditure incurred by them for rendering non-managerial services can be reimbursed to the extent permissible under the law.[20]

There has been a welcome relaxation in the policy on managerial remuneration. The *Eighth Annual Report* states:

The criteria for the scrutiny of such applications were reconsidered by the Board during the year under review. With regard to appointment, no change has been made in the criterion, namely, that of suitability, which will continue to be applied to ensure efficiency management. With regard to remuneration, however, the Company Law Board has decided to adopt a flexible attitude, and restrict its scrutiny mainly to ensure that the ceilings on managerial remuneration adopted by Government are not exceeded except for valid reasons, and that the provisions of the Companies Act in regard to the percentage which managerial remuneration should bear to the net-profit are adhered to. Within these limits, the Company Law Board would prefer to leave decisions about remuneration largely to the management and the shareholders, reserving for its special scrutiny proposals in regard to associates of Managing Agents, as also those for protection of minimum remuneration in cases of absence of or inadequacy of profits. In regard to the latter, the Company Law Board is of the view that protection of minimum remuneration could be justified only for temporary periods, such as the initial period after formation of a company, or during a period of substantial development, or in exceptional period of stress and strain. Protection of minimum remuneration is not contemplated by the Companies Act to be a normal feature of management, and should not, therefore, be treated as such.[21]

And in the *Ninth Annual Report*, the board relaxed the limitation on remuneration of a managing director or manager.

The Board generally continued to follow the criteria for the scrutiny of these applications as mentioned in para 52 of the Eighth Annual Report. In the light of the flexible attitude adopted by the Board in regard to managerial remuneration, it was further decided that the ceiling of Rs 1,20,000/—per annum which was being imposed on the remuneration of Managing/Wholetime Director or Manager, by way of salary, dearness allowance, commission on net profits, etc. (but excluding perquisites), should be relaxed normally by a further amount of Rs 50,000/—that is, to a figure of Rs 1,70,000/—p.a., if the facts and circumstances of the case indicated such relaxation to be justified. In exceptional cases, this enhanced ceiling could be relaxed even further to make marginal adjustments.[22]

Foreign enterprise should note particularly the following statement found in the *Eighth Annual Report:*

Some companies which had some foreign Technicians, whose income was exempt from the payment of Income-tax for a limited period, acting as Managing/Wholetime Directors, applied to the Government under Section 310 of the Act for an increase in their remuneration. While considering such request, the companies concerned were advised to seek the approval in the first instance of the appropriate wing in the Ministry of Industries, which had initially approved their contracts as Technicians, for purposes of exemption from payment of Income-tax, if they wanted the additional remuneration also to be tax-free. The Companies were advised that failing such approval, the additional remuneration could not automatically be deemed to be free of Income-tax.[23]

MANAGING AGENTS

The managing agency system continues to be a controversial subject in India. The government is under considerable pressure from various quarters to abolish the system. It established the Managing Agency Inquiry Committee, headed by Dr. I. G. Patel, economic advisor to the government, to study the matter and make recommendations. Meanwhile, the government has been extremely circumspect in approving new and extending old appointments. In 1965 a great number of appointments came up for renewal. The government extended them in most cases only until the end of 1966 in order not to bind its hand in the event the decision, after the committee's report, is to abolish the system.

The Monopolies Inquiry Commission considered the role of the managing agency system in the concentration of economic power. The commission refrained from making recommendations on the system, in part, doubtless, because another committee had been set up for the purpose. It concluded, however, that the system had contributed substantially to a high degree of concentration of economic power in the hands of a few family groups. The commission gave the following reasons for its position:

Some may enquire why we have made no recommendations as regards the abolition or control of managing agency system, even though we mentioned in an earlier Chapter the important part played by this system in the growth of concentration of economic power. The reasons are more than one. The most important of these is that we are doubtful whether even the total abolition of the managing agency system at the present stage would have any marked effect in curbing the growth of concentration of economic power. We are inclined to believe that even if the managing agency system goes, its place would quickly be taken by some other system of group management, or some other method which it will not be practicable to prevent. Secondly, the question of what action, if any, should be taken as regards managing agency system has to be decided—what action, if any, in addition to what is provided in the Companies Act—not only on a consideration of its effect on concentration of economic power but on full and careful assessment of the effect of any proposed action on the process of Industrial advancement in the country, which is hardly possible for this Commission to undertake. Another consideration which weighed with us was the fact that as recently as 1960 Parliament has carefully considered the question of appropriate action to be taken to control the operation of managing agencies and it seems too early to reopen the question now. Further, it has to be mentioned that the question of the abolition of the managing agency system as regards selected industries is already under the consideration of a Committee appointed by Government.[24]

Dr. I. G. Patel reserved his views because of his participation in the study on the managing agency system. But R. C. Dutt set forth his own views as follows:

Reference has been made in this connection to the system of Managing Agency, though, in my opinion, it would be wrong to regard this system as a cause of concentration. It was, on the other hand, a system devised to facilitate concentration, and should, therefore, be looked upon as an instrument of concentration. It was, however, an important and effective instrument, and it derived one of its main justifications from the alleged shortage of managerial talent. Undoubtedly, there was a shortage of such talent, and in fact to an extent, there is such a shortage even now. A shortage of talent is in fact bound to exist at the initial stages when the field for the exercise of the talent is new, or when the pace of development is so fast that the demand for such talent exceeds supply, in spite of every effort being made to accelerate supply. This is a difficulty which cannot be regarded as abnormal in the process of industrialisation. It has to be met. A defect of the Managing Agency system is that it makes no attempt to meet the difficulty. On the contrary by concentrating power in the hands of a few it denies opportunity to others to develop managerial talent. The justification of the Managing Agency system does not, therefore, lie in the shortage of managerial talent in the country. It lies elsewhere. The system was introduced by the British rulers of India for the purpose of controlling as much of the industrial sector as possible with the limited number of their nationals available in this country. It certainly served that purpose. Later, it was adopted by Indian industrialists who were first in the field, and it helped them to maintain their pioneering advantage. While from the British national or imperial point of view the system could be justified just because it helped to concentrate economic power in their hands, from the Indian point of view this could no longer by itself provide adequate justification for it. In any case, the Managing Agency system has always been a potent factor for the concentration of economic power, and it still continues to be so.

Reasons have been adduced in this Chapter why no recommendation has been made for the abolition of the system. I do not agree with the first reason mentioned that "even if the managing agency goes, its place would be taken by some other system of group management, or some other method which it will not be practicable to prevent." With due respect, this is in my opinion a counsel of despair. If other methods appear which are harmful they will have to be dealt with, but if the abolition of the system of Managing Agency is considered necessary in the interests of the country, it cannot be allowed to continue merely because some alternative method equally harmful may be devised to take its place. I do not also agree with another reason, which has been recorded in the Report, namely, that since the matter was considered by the Government in 1960 "it seems too early to re-open the matter now." The problem of concentration of economic power has attracted attention in recent years, and has assumed importance on the eve of the Fourth Five-Year Plan when a further massive effort to accelerate the pace of industrialisation is envisaged. In this context, a fresh look at the problem is, in my opinion, entirely justified.

I agree, however, as stated in the Report that a recommendation about the future of the Managing Agency system must be based "not only on its effect on concentration of economic power but on full and careful assessment of the effects of any proposed action on the process of industrial advancement in the country. . . ." I also agree that since Government have already appointed another Committee to consider this matter, it should be left to that Committee to make specific recommendations. While, therefore, I agree that this Commission need make no recommendation in this respect, I think the conclusion should be recorded that the Managing Agency system is a potent instrument of concentration of economic power, and that to the extent concentration has to be discouraged this instrument must be dealt with.[25]

In support of his views Mr. Dutt indicated the degree of control exercised through a common managing agency or agencies of the five large industrial groups:

Tata	74%
Birla	82%
Martin-Burn	91%
Bangur	45%
Thapar	58%

The system seems to be fading away by itself as most new industrial undertakings prefer board management with or without a managing director. The restrictions imposed by the Companies Act have, doubtless, contributed to this trend in no small measure. Before the 1956 act, there were 3,944 agencies managing the affairs of 5,055 companies. Since then the number of operating companies has increased, but at the end of 1964-65 only 860 managing agents managed 1,236 companies. Equally significant is the fact disclosed in the Reserve Bank studies that managing agency commissions declined from 12.6 per cent in 1950-51 to 4.2 per cent in 1962-63 as a proportion of gross profits.

The reasons for the decline are many and complex. They have, perhaps, been summed up best by the *Economic Times* in the following editorial:

There is no doubt that the influence of the managing agency system in the corporate sector has been waning fast, perhaps faster than what was visualised by policy makers.

Moreover, the whole pattern of industrial growth and the diversification of industrial production in recent years have called for a new category of talent in the management field. Modern production techniques, the induction of foreign capital and foreign technical know-how and the emergence of a new managerial class with a considerable degree of training and sophistication have already brought about a silent revolution in the management field. This has inevitably relegated the traditional managing agency into the background, especially in new areas of industrial advancement. This is a trend which will be further accelerated when the new institutes for management studies in Bombay, Calcutta, Ahmedabad and Delhi turn out more and more accomplished management executives. While the scope of the managing agencies has thus generally shrunk on the management side, their role in financing has also tended to contract because of the magnitude of investments involved in modern projects and the multiplicity of institutions set up for industrial financing.

With this unmistakable evidence of the managing agency system gradually fading out in importance, it is legitimate to ask whether there is any need for drastic measures that may disrupt confidence in vital sectors of the corporate economy.[26]

Nonetheless, the government decided in July, 1966, to abolish the managing agency system in five industries—cotton and jute textiles, cement, paper, and sugar—pursuant to its power under Section 324 of the Companies Act.

In the *Seventh Annual Report,* the department sets forth some of the considerations borne in mind in approving managing agencies pursuant to the criteria provided in Section 326.

(i) Whether having regard to their qualifications and business experience and any organization maintained by them, the proposed managing agents are properly equipped to render comprehensive services to the managed company;

(ii) Whether the partners or directors of the proposed managing agents are already connected with the management of other companies or otherwise pre-occupied with their own business which would leave them little or no time to devote to the affairs of the managed company. Where the person proposed for appointment as managing agent is already managing several companies, the application will be carefully examined to see whether he would be in a position to do justice to the efficient management of any more companies;

(iii) Whether the past performance of the person proposed to be appointed has been good and beneficial to the company concerned;

(iv) Where it has been found that an existing managing agent was sub-delegating most of his powers and functions to salaried executives of the managed company, and thus failed to render sufficient services to the latter, he could hardly be regarded as a fit and proper person for being entrusted with the management of the company for a further term;

(v) Whether the change-over to management by managing agent from any other existing form of management would materially benefit the managed company and result in the better management of its affairs without imposing undue financial burden on it. In other words, the need for the proposed change-over should be fully justified to the satisfaction of the Commission and the Government;

(vi) Whether having regard to the small size, meagre financial resources and the nature of the business of a company, it would not be in its interest to adopt any other form of management.[27]

SELLING AGENTS

During recent years, foreign enterprise has encountered more frequently a selling agency as part of the planned business organization for the proposed project. The rise of the selling agency coincides with the decline of the managing agency. Indian entrepreneurs resort to a selling agency as a facile means to enhance their managerial remuneration otherwise severely restricted by the Companies Act. Foreign collaborators, particularly those with substantial equity participation, view the selling agency usually with considerable dismay, as it enables the Indian partners to participate in the profits before or in addition to payment of dividends. At the same time, it must be granted that a selling agency can perform a useful function of selling and distribution that would otherwise have to be done by the company.

Section 294 prohibits the appointment of sole selling agents for a term exceeding five years at a time. At the same time, it empowers the central government whenever it deems fit to

require the company to furnish to it such information regarding the terms and conditions of the appointment of sole selling agent as it considers necessary for the purpose of determining whether or not such terms and conditions are prejudicial to the interests of the company [and] if after perusal of the information . . . the Central Government is of the opinion that the terms and conditions of appointment are prejudicial to the interests of the company, the Central Government may, by order, make such variations in those terms and conditions as would, in its opinion, make them no longer prejudicial to the interests of the company.[28]

Where more than one selling agent is involved, the government may declare them to be, in effect, sole selling agents if warranted by the circumstances and likewise reorder the terms and conditions of the appointment.[29]

Former managing agents can be appointed sole selling agents only with the approval of the government during a period of three years after termination of the managing agency.[30] The 1965 act prohibits the payment of compensation to sole selling agents for loss of office in certain cases, such as fraud or gross negligence, failure of approval by the company in general meeting, and as a result of a reconstruction or amalgamation of the company.[31]

This new trend in business organization has been viewed with considerable concern by the Company Law Board. During the three-year period ending March 31, 1965, information was requested from forty-one companies and changes in the terms and conditions of appointment ordered in about half of the cases. The greatest proportion of cases were in the textile and sugar industries. The comment in the *Eighth Annual Report* to the effect that "company law does not provide an effective deterrent for this undesirable trend in the corporate sector" is interesting. It may presage further restrictions in the future.

CORPORATE LOANS AND INVESTMENTS

The restrictions on intercorporate loans were increased by the 1965 act. Section 370 now prescribes that all intercorporate loans require a special resolution, except loans made to other companies not under the same management that do not exceed 10 per cent of the subscribed capital and free reserves of the lending company. Prior government approval is, further, required if the aggregate of the loans made to all bodies corporate exceed 30 per cent of the subscribed capital and free reserves of the lending company in the case of all such bodies corporate not under the same management, and 20 per cent in the case of all other corporate bodies under the same management as the lending company. The new provision conforms more closely to the restriction on intercorporate investments.

PROTECTION OF PUBLIC AND MINORITY INTERESTS

The main thrust of the 1963 and 1965 acts, particularly the former, was to strengthen the powers of the central government to intervene in corporate affairs in the public interest. Sections 397-98 and 408-9 were amended to include remedial action by the courts or government if the affairs of a company "are being conducted in a manner prejudicial to public interest." A new section 388B was added which empowers the central government to refer cases to the Companies Tribunal for decision, declaring persons as unfit to hold the offices of director or other positions connected with the management of companies.

It is too early to comment on the implications of these changes in the Companies Act. It is to be noted that before the 1963 act, the courts were already reading the public interest into its interpretations of sections 397-98.[32] The impact of the Bose report on the Indian public, however, impelled the government to make clear that the public interest was to be injected into the administration of company law by the courts and administration. The sweep of the new provisions is broad. Their interpretation and administration by the Company Law Board, Companies Tribunal, and courts will be watched with considerable interest inside and outside India.

An interesting case is already underway—an outgrowth of the Bose report. One of the companies under the control of the Dalmia-Jain group was Bennett, Coleman & Co., Ltd., which publishes the influential *Times of India, Economic Times, Illustrated Weekly,* and other publications. The government first appointed an inspector, S. Prakash Chopra who is a chartered accountant, to investigate the affairs of Bennett, Coleman pursuant to section 237 of the act. Mr. Chopra submitted a report of more than two hundred pages. In addition to a compilation of intercompany and personal loans, investments, and other transactions, Mr. Chopra complains of obstruction of his investigation by company officials and employees.

After the investigation, the government moved the Companies Tribunal to oust Shanti Prasad Jain, and/or his wife, Rama Jain, who succeeded him in September, 1964, during the pendency of the action, as chairman of the board of Bennett, Coleman, pursuant to sections 388B, 398, 401, and 403 of the act, as persons unfit to manage the company's affairs. An interim order was requested to appoint a special officer to manage the company pending the tribunal's decision. The Companies Tribunal passed the interim order on October 29, 1964, appointing Dr. R. C. Cooper, a renowned chartered accountant of Bombay, as chairman of the board pending the disposition of the main action. The tribunal ordered, further, that no resolution of the board could take effect unless it had the consent of Dr. Cooper. The other directors were, however, given a right to appeal to the tribunal against Dr. Cooper's action.

The central government also exercised its power under section 408 by appointing two directors to the board. This received the sanction of the tribunal although such sanction is not required by law.

The tribunal has not yet turned its attention to the merits of the case. After the interim order, the defendants set out to challenge the jurisdiction of the tribunal and initiated other peripheral legal actions typical of such litigation the world over. These are now being disposed of by the courts. Among others was a plea of contempt against some of the daily newspapers—the *Times of India,* the *Statesman, The Hindustan Times,* and others—for publishing and prominently displaying some details of the petition filed by the government and a summary of the Chopra report. The inclusion of the *Times of India* in the charge is somewhat ironical.

It is interesting to observe in this connection that the Monopolies Commission noted the control of the nation's press by the large industrial groups. Shanti Prasad Jain controls the *Times of India* publications, and the Birlas control the *Hindustan Times* and allied publications including the *Eastern Economist.* Ramnath Goenka controls the chain of Express papers. Only a few newspapers are free of big business control. Although the commission refrained from making any recommendation, it expressed the need for the existence of more newspapers free of business control.[33] R. C. Dutt, however, deplored more vigorously the control of the press by big business.[34]

During the past few years, the courts continued to entertain cases under sections 397-98. As required by section 400, the government received notices of such suits in thirty-two cases in 1963-64 and seventeen cases in 1964-65. Representations by the Company Law Board were filed in eight and five cases, respectively.

Several important points of law were decided by the high courts. In one case it was held that in an application under sections 397-98, all material facts must be pleaded at the start and if the allegations do not make out a cause of action, facts arising subsequent to the filing of the application or further evidence by affidavits cannot be used to correct the deficiency.[35] Another high court held that a majority as well as a minority of shareholders can seek relief under sections 397-98 in appropriate cases.[36] In another important decision, the court held that action under sections 397-98 could be sought even if the company was no longer in active business.[37] A single act of oppression was held sufficient to justify relief; the oppression need not necessarily be continuous or protracted.[38]

Petitions for relief under sections 408-9 appear to have subsided the past two years. The 1963 act authorized the government to act on its own initiative under section 408. As already noted above, it appointed two directors to the board of Bennett, Coleman, in addition to its action against the company management under section 388B and 398.

RECONSTRUCTION AND AMALGAMATION

The 1965 act amended section 394 to provide that no compromise or arrangement for company reorganization may be approved by the court unless the Company Law Board, registrar or liquidator, as the case may be, reports that "the affairs of the company have not been conducted in a manner prejudicial to the interests of its members or to public interest."[39] The government already possessed the power to provide for compulsory amalgamation of companies in the public interest.[40]

GOVERNMENT COMPANIES

The number of government companies at work as of March 31, 1965, was 183. In juxtaposition there were 26,653 nongovernment companies, of which 5,978 were public companies.

The Orissa project is interesting in this connection. Its purpose is to assist private entrepreneurs, with know-how and managerial ability but short on capital, to establish industries in the state. Government companies are formed with the Orissa government holding 90 per cent of the share capital and the private entrepreneurs 10 per cent. The board is composed of four government directors, with the private entrepreneur as the fifth and also the managing director of the company. The scheme envisages eventual transfer of the government shares to the private entrepreneur as the company attains profitable operations. The surplus profits, after providing for a minimum dividend and essential reserves, are made available to the entrepreneur for purchasing the government shares.

In order to facilitate such transfer of ownership to the private entrepreneur, the Orissa government proposed to convert part of their equity shares to loan capital. Such a conversion would amount to a reduction of capital and require sanction of the court each time under section 100. The central government, therefore, exempted the Orissa government companies under the scheme from the requirements of section 100 as it is empowered to do by section 620, requiring that these companies obtain confirmation instead of the central government for the capital reduction.

The Orissa project is worth watching, as it may prove an effective means of facilitating private sector projects in the present tight and forbidding capital market. The essence of the scheme is to enable private entrepreneurs to build their equity out of the success of the new industrial undertaking.

FOREIGN COMPANIES

The 1965 act eased the requirement on reporting changes in the company's affairs required by section 593 by omitting changes in the circumstances of the directors and secretary, such as directorships held, occupational changes, and the like.

The Company Law Board continued to grant limited exemptions from the requirements on filing its accounts with the registrar. In one case, however, it required a foreign company to file a supplementary abstract of the accounts in rupees when the Indian shareholders complained that they found it difficult to follow the reports made out in a foreign currency.

X

Capital Issues Control

There have been some policy changes in capital issues control in the light of the moribund capital market during the past few years. The preference-equity share ratio was relaxed to 1:3 in view of the comeback of preference shares as a popular security. The debt-equity ratio has also been relaxed in appropriate cases. Underwriting commissions have been increased from 2.5 to 3 per cent.

The buoyant stock market that existed until 1962 is gone, and it is doubtful that a similar market will soon return. The situation today causes the underwriters to hold the new capital issues for long periods. Since new issues now drop in value until the enterprise comes into profitability, the underwriters try to hedge their portfolios by matching equity shares with preference shares and debentures. A typical underwriting today will consist of half equity and half preference shares. Normally the Indian entrepreneur and his foreign collaborator subscribe half the equity capital. The result is a 1:3 preference-equity share ratio.

Eventually, it is hoped, the new issues will be sold to the public by the underwriters. Meanwhile, the underwriters will be strained for funds to continue underwriting. In the end, the government will be expected to keep them supplied with rupee loans if it desires the private sector to start new industrial undertakings.

XI

Taxation

The two Finance Acts of 1965 made fundamental changes in the corporate tax structure. The most significant, perhaps, was the introduction of new tax concessions in the form of the tax certificate schemes to stimulate private investment, production, and exports. Existing tax concessions were enhanced. There was also a simplification and liberalization of personal taxation of both residents and nonresidents. The Finance Act of 1966 made similar profound changes. It simplified and rearranged the rate structure resulting in an over-all increase in corporate and personal taxation. Two basic changes were made in taxation of dividends. The 7.5 per cent supertax on profits paid out as dividends was made applicable only with respect to dividends in excess of 10 per cent on paid up capital. Bonus shares were freed of capital gains tax until sold or transferred by the shareholder, and the 12.5 per cent supertax payable by the company on an issue of bonus shares was repealed. Finally, the controversial Expenditure Tax was repealed, not suspended as before during the period April 1, 1962, to March 31, 1964. There was also further simplification and liberalization of various tax provisions. The details follow.

CORPORATE RATE STRUCTURE

Indian companies and foreign corporations distributing dividends in India pay a corporation income tax at the rate of 55 per cent. Closely held companies are taxed at the rate of 60 per cent, except that industrial companies (mainly engaged in manufacturing, processing, construction of ships, mining, or power generation or distribution) are taxed at 55 per cent on the first Rs 1 million of taxable income.[1]

Closely held companies are defined as those in which the public is not substantially interested. Private companies are *ipso facto* in this tax category because their shares are not available for public subscription. Public companies fall into the category if 5 or fewer persons own 50 per cent, or 60 per cent in the case of industrial companies, or more of the voting shares. A secondary definition states that a company in which the public is substantially interested is a company in which 40 or 50 per cent, as the case may be, of the voting shares are owned by the government, government companies, or the public. A special supertax is levied on closely held industrial companies failing to distribute 45 per cent of their profits to shareholders by way of dividends. Trading companies are required to distribute 60 per cent and investment companies 90 per cent of their profits to avoid the supertax.[2]

The 1966 act exempts foreign corporations from this supertax.[3] In practice it was not applied to foreign companies though the law was unclear. The 1966 act has now clarified the situation.

Dividends paid by an Indian company to another Indian company or foreign corporation are taxable at the rate of 25 per cent to the corporate shareholder. Dividends from a closely held Indian company to a foreign corporate shareholder are taxed at 15 per cent.

A special supertax of 7.5 per cent on profits paid out as dividends in excess of 10 per cent on paid up capital is imposed on the company paying the dividend.[4] Bonus shares or stock dividends do not attract supertax or capital gains tax as before at the time of issue.[5]

The surtax on company profits was reduced from 40 to 35 per cent by the Finance Act of 1966, and the super profits tax was repealed. It had been suspended since April 1, 1964.[6]

Foreign companies are now required to pay income tax at the rate of 70 per cent.[7] Foreign collaboration income tax rates remain unchanged. Royalties and technical fees under approved agreements are taxed at 50 per cent. Dividends received from Indian companies are taxed at 25 per cent, 15 per cent from closely held companies. Interest on approved foreign loans is tax exempt.

The 1966 act extended similar concessionary rates to Indian companies entering into foreign collaboration abroad. Dividends, royalties, and fees derived from such collaboration are taxed at the rate of 25 per cent.[8]

An over-all limitation of 70 per cent on the above rates was provided in the Finance Act of 1965.[9]

TAX CONCESSIONS

High priority industries were granted a 10 per cent rebate (reducing the corporate tax from 50 to 45 per cent) by the 1964 act. The 1966 act changed this concession to an 8 per cent exemption of otherwise taxable profits from tax.[10] High priority industries were redefined to include those listed in the Fifth Schedule of the Income Tax Act, 1961. Tea, newsprint, and printing machinery were added to the Fifth Schedule for this purpose.

High priority industries specified in the Fifth Schedule were granted a higher 35 per cent development rebate for new machinery and equipment installed during the April 1, 1965, to March 31, 1970, period and 25 per cent thereafter. New ships are still entitled to a 40 per cent development rebate, and the development rebate reserve was reduced to 50 per cent by the 1966 act. All other industries receive development rebate at the rate of 20 per cent until March 31, 1970, and 15 per cent thereafter.[11] The tea plantation industry was extended a special development allowance by the 1965 act of 40 per cent of the cost of planting tea bushes in a new area and 20 per cent of the cost of replanting tea bushes in old areas. The allowance was further enhanced to 50 and 30 per cent, respectively, by the 1966 act.[12]

Two tax rebates for the purpose of stimulating exports were provided by the Finance Act of 1965. A rebate of 10 per cent of the amount of income tax payable on profits derived from the export of goods was extended all exporters. Another rebate was granted manufacturers who exported the manufactured goods or sold them to another for export to the extent of 2 per cent of the sales proceeds of the goods. This rebate was limited to manufactured articles listed in the First Schedule of the Industries Act, 1951.[13] These concessions were terminated in June, 1966.

Further concessions were made specifically to foreign enterprise. Where a foreign company or individual derives capital gain from the transfer of shares in an Indian company and reinvests the sales proceeds in an investment approved by the government within two years of the transfer, the capital gains tax is waived or refunded.[14] The interest on nonresident accounts is exempt from tax.[15] Nonresidents are exempt from tax on any security approved by the central government by notification in the Official Gazette.[16]

Foreign technicians are allowed an additional three years of freedom from tax on income tax paid by their employer, provided that government approval is obtained for such extension of employment. In other words, a foreign technician may now secure tax exemption for three years and freedom from taxation on the tax paid by his employer for five years thereafter.[17]

A noteworthy tax concession was introduced by the Finance Act, 1965. Companies are now allowed a deduction for expenditures incurred for promoting family planning among their employees. Where the expenditure is capital in nature the deduction is to be spread over five years.

TAX CREDIT CERTIFICATES

The Finance Act, 1965, introduced the practice of granting subsidies through the tax system for various economic development purposes. The amount of tax credit must first be adjusted against any existing tax liability or any tax liability arising within a year of presentation of the tax certificate to the income tax office for redemption. The excess over such tax liability, if any, is refunded in cash. The tax credits are free of income tax.

The Finance Act, 1965, provides for five tax credit certificate schemes. They are the following, some with special features and qualifications.

1. *Tax credit certificates for investment in specified equity shares.*[18] Any individual or joint Hindu family subscribing and paying for an "eligible issue" of equity shares of a company is entitled to a tax credit certificate calculated on the amount of the investment in the financial year payment for the shares is made and for each of the three succeeding financial years during which the shares are held at the rate of 5 per cent on the first Rs 15,000, 3 per cent on the next Rs 10,000, and 2 per cent on the next Rs 10,000. The maximum credit available in any one year is Rs 1,250 on the total investment of Rs 35,000 or more. If the shares are sold during the period, the credit is granted in proportion to the investment held at the end of the financial year.

The scope of the "eligible issue" of equity shares and the procedure for obtaining the tax credit certificates are to be promulgated by the central government. In December, 1965, the central government announced that the "eligible issue" will include shares of an Indian company manufacturing or processing, or proposing to do so, articles included in the First Schedule to the Industries Act, 1951. The issue must be made on or after December 24, 1964.

2. *Tax credit certificates for dispersal of industries from urban areas.*[19] A tax credit certificate is granted a public company to provide relief from capital gains tax arising from the transfer of land and buildings in relocating its industrial undertaking from an urban to another area. The certificate is to be granted in the amount of expenditure incurred by the company in acquiring land and buildings in the new area and shifting its machinery and equipment to that area up to the amount of the capital gains tax incurred in the relocation. No refund of tax is possible under this scheme.

Urban areas are to be designated by the government having regard for such factors as population, industrial concentration, congestion, and related factors.

3. *Tax credit certificates based on increased tax liability.*[20] A company manufacturing articles listed in the First Schedule of the Industries Act, 1951, is entitled to a tax credit calculated at 20 per cent of the increased income tax liability, subject to a limit of 10 per cent of its total liability, over its income tax liability for the base year 1965-66, during each of the five assessment years from 1966-67 to 1970-71. Where only a part of the company's profits derive from such manufacture, the tax credit is to be reckoned only with reference to such profits.

4. *Tax credit certificates for increased production.*[21] Any person (whether a company or not), who manufactures certain goods specified by the government during any one or more of the five assessment years 1965-66 to 1969-70, in excess of the base year 1964-65, is entitled to a tax credit certificate up to 25 per cent of the central excise duty payable by him on the excess production. The peculiar structure of this tax credit based on the excise duty instead of the income tax is for the purpose of limiting this tax concession to stimulating the production of essential commodities. Most essential commodities are subject to the central excise duty, but not many other commodities are, which limits this subsidy to essential commodities. The subsidy derives from the fact that the excise duty is passed on to the consumer. Hence, partial rebate results in a pure gain to the manufacturer.

The goods eligible for and the amount of the tax credit to be granted are to be specified by the government. On November 5, 1965, the government issued the rules, procedure, and forms for this tax credit scheme.[22] Earlier in August, the government announced the following commodities and percentage of rebate eligible for tax credit.

Cement	25 per cent
Newsprint	25 per cent
Caustic soda	20 per cent
Soda ash	20 per cent
Paper	15 per cent

5. *Tax credit certificates for increased exports.*[23] Any person (whether a company or not) who exports any goods or merchandise after February 28, 1965, specified by the central government, is entitled to a tax credit certificate at the rates specified, not exceeding 15 per cent of the sales proceeds of the exports. The Finance Act (No. 2), 1965, provides that "sales proceeds" do not include freight or insurance incurred in connection with the export. The tax credit certificate is conditioned on the receipt of the sales proceeds in India in accordance with the Foreign Exchange Regulation Act, 1947, and the rules thereunder. Unlike the other schemes, a refund is payable only after adjustment against any existing income tax liability of the recipient of the certificate at the time when he produces it to the appropriate tax authority for redemption. It need not be offset against any tax liability arising during the ensuing twelve months.

The central government notified a scheme for this tax credit on August 17, 1965, which sets forth the procedure and forms for obtaining the certificates and specifies the commodities and rates on which the certificates will be granted.[24] Some twenty-two commodities are listed with rates ranging from 2 to 15 per cent. For example, a 2 per cent tax credit is specified for loose tea, other than green tea, jute products, and cashew nuts; 5 per cent for green tea, packaged tea, and calcined magnesite; 10 per cent for iron ore, coal, fresh fruits, tiles, and other items; and 15 per cent for manganese ore, mineral ores, mica powder, ferro manganese, and alcoholic beverages. Exports to Nepal, Bhutan, and Sikkim are not eligible for the tax credit.

The tax credit scheme for exports was terminated in July, 1966. As noted earlier a straight monetary subsidy to promote exports was adopted instead.

It is to be noted that the tax credit certificate schemes delegate considerable authority to the central government. Items and rates may be expected to change from time to time by notification of the government. Such flexibility is, perhaps, desirable for the administration of such a sensitive program of economic incentives, though some in the private sector will find it disturbing.

OTHER CHANGES AND AMENDMENTS

The five-year tax holiday for new industrial undertakings to the extent of 6 per cent of the capital employed was extended for another five-year period up to March 31, 1971, by the Finance Act (No. 2), 1965. This tax concession has now been available without interruption since April 1, 1948.[25]

The Finance Act, 1966, provides for the amortization of the cost of acquiring a patent or copyright for purposes of business over a fourteen-year period or the unexpired life, whichever is less, in equal annual installments.[26] Where the patent or copyright is sold, any excess of the sales proceeds over the unamortized amount of the cost of acquisition must be returned as income and any shortfall may be taken as a deduction in the year of sale.

The 1965 act restored the five-year exemption from Wealth Tax of equity investment in new industrial undertakings. The concession is applicable to companies issuing capital for the first time after February 28, 1965.[27]

FOREIGN PERSONNEL

Personal taxation was considerably simplified by the 1965 act. A single rate was adopted instead of the previous combination of income tax and super-tax rates. The surcharge was retained.

The 1966 act, however, imposed a special surcharge of 10 per cent on the amount of income tax and surcharge on both earned and unearned incomes. The exemptions and personal allowances were raised by Rs 500 in each case.

The greatest change was made in the taxation of nonresidents.[28] In the past, a nonresident was charged at an over-all rate of 48.37 per cent or higher if the applicable super-tax rate exceeded 19 per cent. He was given the option, however, to declare his earned income and pay either (a) the tax payable on his Indian income as if he were a resident, or (b) a proportionate tax on his Indian income at the rate applicable to his world income, whichever was higher. An election so made was binding for all succeeding years.

The 1965 act provides that a nonresident will be charged tax on his Indian income at the rates applicable to residents, without any reference to his world income, but without any personal allowances or exemption.

Concurrently, the withholding rates were changed. Deduction on salary income is at the average rate applicable to the total salary income. On all other income it is 30 per cent, except interest on government securities where a lower 15 per cent rate applies. Previously, deduction at source was at the rate of 48.37 per cent or more.

A few other concessions have been extended to foreigners, in addition to the important one concerning foreign technicians. A professor or teacher who is not a citizen of India is exempt from tax on his remuneration from a university or other educational institution in India for a period of three years. Thereafter, he continues to be exempt on the perquisites represented by such payment for an additional two years. The contract of employment must have prior approval by the central government, and the professor or teacher must not have been a resident in India during any of the four years preceding his arrival in India for the exempt employment.[29]

A stipend paid from a foreign source to an individual who is not a citizen of India for undertaking research work in India under a program approved by the central government is exempt from tax for a period of two years.[30]

An education allowance against income tax is permitted an individual, not a citizen of but resident in India, on expenditures incurred by him for the full-time education of his children under twenty-one years of age in a university, college, or school outside India. The rebate, calculated at the average rate applicable to his total income, is limited to Rs 2,000 per child or 25 per cent of the taxpayers' taxable income, whichever is less.[31]

COMMODITY TAXATION

Commodity taxation, particularly import and excise duties, continues as the main source of revenue. Both have been considerably enhanced by the 1965 and 1966 acts. Increased import duties imposed primarily by the Finance Act (No. 2), 1965, have been resorted to for the equally important purpose of curtailing imports in the face of the worsening foreign exchange shortage. Excise duties are resorted to also for the additional purpose of restraining consumption. Much was made of this point in the presentation of the 1966-67 budget to parliament.[32] Where it was found, however, that the excise duty proved so burdensome that it depressed the particular industry, as in the case of rayon yarn and staple fiber in 1964, the rate was reduced.

The Finance Act, 1966, increased the central sales tax on interstate sales from 2 to 3 per cent. At the same time, the ceiling on state sales taxes on goods of special importance in interstate commerce, like cotton, cotton yarn, hides and skins, oilseeds, jute, coal, iron, and steel, was raised from 2 to 3 per cent. The new rates are effective as of July 1, 1966. The revenues from the central sales tax are allocated to the states.

These constant changes in corporate taxation are, perhaps, the most persistently disturbing feature in India for foreign enterprise. At times it appears as if the tax on companies depends upon the personal whim of the finance minister. A closer study, however, reveals that there has been a consistent policy throughout of taxing about 50 per cent of company profits with substantial concessions to stimulate new investment, increased production, and, more recently, greater exports. The skirmishing has been mostly on the periphery.

The taxation of foreign collaboration income (dividends, royalties, and fees) has undergone constant improvement and can be considered satisfactory at this time. This is particularly true of an American company that finds the Indian tax about equal to the U.S.A. income tax for purposes of its foreign tax credit. The main disturbance then is over the constant changes in the taxation of Indian companies.

The complexity of the corporate tax structure in India renders it almost impossible to project the incidence of tax, particularly with respect to new industrial undertakings. Too many variable and countervailing provisions are involved. Experience reveals, however, that an Indian company engaged in a priority industry is unlikely to pay an effective rate of tax exceeding 50 per cent unless its profits before tax exceed 40 per cent of capital invested. In the case of a new industrial undertaking on the priority list, encountering the usual starting up losses and availing itself of all the tax concessions for new enterprises, the average effective rate over the first ten years of operation is not likely to exceed 25 per cent. Indian companies outside this favored realm may find themselves approaching the maximum effective rate of 70 per cent.

Whether corporate taxation in India is excessive as is often alleged, is difficult to assess. It is obviously meaningless to assert that the tax is too high without relating it to the profitability of Indian companies. The fact that most Indian companies are able to pay dividends in excess of 10 per cent on paid-up capital or in excess of 6 per cent on market value of the shares after reinvesting about 40 per cent of after-tax profits would appear to belie the charge that corporate taxation in India is excessive.

XII

Industrial Property Rights

After a decade of procrastination on basic reform of the patent law, a bill to amend the Indian Patents and Designs Act, 1911, was introduced in the Lok Sabha on September 21, 1965. Considerable uncertainty and anxiety was generated regarding the proposed amendments the past few years. Nothing has perhaps disturbed foreign enterprise more on the Indian scene in recent times than the proposed amendments.

The bill purports to be based mainly on Justice Ayyangar's recommendations and "incorporates a few further changes in the light of further examination, particularly with reference to patents for food, medicine and drugs."[1] It is these "few further changes" that proved most disturbing.

The bill makes a sharp departure from the old law contained in the 1911 act. The salient new provisions are the following:

1. The term of patent is reduced from sixteen to fourteen years, and in the case of foods, medicines, and drugs, to ten years from the date of the patent. The term of existing patents in this field is also limited to ten years from the date of the patent.

2. Patent protection in the case of foods, medicines, drugs, substances produced by chemical process (including alloys), optical glass, semi-conductors, and inter-metallic compounds will be granted only for the process of manufacture and not for the manufactured product.

3. All patents for food, medicines, drugs, and chemical procedures shall be deemed to be endorsed with the words "License of right." This means that any person shall be entitled to use the patent subject to the royalty payable under the compulsory license provisions.

4. The royalty payable to the patentee with respect to patents

endorsed with the words "License of right" shall in no case exceed 4 per cent of the net ex-factory bulk price of the product.

5. A patented product may be imported by the government from anywhere for its own use (or the use of any dispensary, hospital, or other medical institution maintained or designated by the government in the case of patented medicine or drug) without infringement of the patent. This permission is intended for research and development and not commercial purposes.

6. Any interested person, or the government, may apply to the high court for revocation of a patent on broader grounds than at present but not merely for non-use. The patent may, however, be revoked by the court on grounds of refusal by the patentee to comply with a request of the central government to use the patent on reasonable terms for purposes of government, including government undertakings and such classes of private sector undertakings as the government may designate. The central government's right of revocation in the public interest, after giving the patentee an opportunity to be heard, already in the existing act, is further clarified and augmented with safeguards.

7. Finally, the controller is empowered to revoke a patent after the expiration of two years where a compulsory license has been granted or the endorsement "License of right" has been made, but the reasonable requirements of the public with respect to the patent have not been satisfied. This provision contains Justice Ayyangar's recommendation to back up compulsory licensing with a power of revocation to induce patentees to transmit to licensees the know-how and technical assistance required to work effectively the naked patent.

The remainder of the bill proceeds to rectify deficiencies in the existing law, strengthen the review and enforcement machinery, and clarify contentious areas of the case law on patents. While the bill incorporates most of Justice Ayyangar's recommendations, it also departs from them in many respects. For instance, Justice Ayyangar believed strongly in the patent system and felt that the term of a patent should be sixteen years. On the other hand, he did question whether "inventions relating to articles of food and medicine" should be patentable as distinguished from the processes to produce the articles. He based his conclusion on the experience he found in most other countries of the world, many of which refuse even to patent the processes for food and medicine.[2] "Barring the U.S.A., there are few countries in the world," he found, "that do not have special provisions as regards the patentability of inventions in respect of articles of food and medicine."[3] Justice Ayyangar did not, however, recommend cutting down the period on the process patents to ten years. Justice Ayyangar opposed any limitation on royalty payable for compulsory licenses because it was not feasible to fix a uniform royalty that would be reasonable to each and every patentee.

Reducing the term of patents to fourteen years and ten years in the case of food, medicine, and drug processes is open to question. The term of patent varies from country to country, but generally ranges between fifteen and twenty years. The starting dates also vary. Sometimes it is the date of application, the date of grant, or the date of publication. Two other countries, Nicaragua and Venezuela, provide ten-year terms. Many underdeveloped countries, however, provide for twenty-year patent terms.

The short ten-year term overlooks the fact that it takes several years to develop the commercial application of most pharmaceutical processes. Hence, the effective period of protection is much shorter, if any, in most cases. This will prove a disincentive to research, experimentation, and innovation in the food, medicine, and drug field as the country progresses toward self-sufficiency in the food processing and pharmaceutical industries. Foreign companies will not, of course, be effected in their research efforts outside India, but they will be more reluctant to bring the fruits of their research to India.

Rendering only the process, not the product, patentable in the food, medicine, drug, and chemical fields appears also contra-trend, particularly in the industrialized countries of Europe. The U.S.A. has always permitted patents for products. Justice Ayyangar based his recommendations on the earlier situation in Europe, pointing particularly to the German patent law of 1877 that permits chemical process patents only as conducive to the early development of the German chemical industry.[4] It is felt that India requires similar freedom for its nascent chemical and pharmaceutical industries at this stage of its industrialization.

The royalty ceiling under compulsory licensing would appear superfluous. It is obviously motivated by the desire to conserve foreign exchange, but the government already possesses sufficient legal and administrative control over royalty payments under the Industries and Foreign Exchange Control Acts. Although the ceiling does not appear more restrictive than the limits imposed under the industrial licensing procedure, its unnecessary inclusion will tend to aggravate the unfavorable reaction of foreign enterprise to the new patent law.

In view of the broad implications and controversial nature of the proposed changes, Parliament referred the bill to a select committee for hearings and study.

The annual report of the Patent Office for 1964 reflects some rise in indigenous inventions and designs. The number of applications involving inventions were 5,676 and 5,705, respectively, for 1963 and 1964. Applications of Indian origin comprised 878 and 902, respectively, during the two years. About 15 per cent originated in India in contrast to 10 per cent or less earlier. Applications for designs originating in India, however, comprised 97 per cent of the total.

Textile technology and design headed the list of domestic applications. Indian research organizations developed inventions on finishing cellulosic fibers and measuring moisture content of yarn. In the chemical industry Indian inventors made contributions in the preparation of polysaccharides, guinacridones, vanillin, benzoic acid, glycolic acid, dehydrated cellulose, sulfur dyes, cracking of hydrocarbons, recovery of essential oils and thermosetting compositions. In metallurgy, Indian inventors made innovations in the extraction of gold and silver, soldering alloys, aluminum alloys, molybdenum alloys, and smelting furnaces. A new process for pipes, melting metal by electric arc, minimizing contamination during casting, boxless molds, corrosion-resistant compositions, and hot dip tinning of strips were subjects of other inventions originating in India.

In the field of mechanical engineering, inventions of Indian origin related to pumps, bicycles, engines, metal working, marine propulsion, typewriters, and automobile tires. An appreciable number of inventions relating to meters and batteries originated in India. In food and agriculture, a number of Indian inventions involved agricultural implements and food processing.

Over-all the chemical industry continued to provide the largest number of patent applications, particularly processes for the preparation of organic compounds useful in pharmaceuticals, dyestuffs, resins, and polymers. Most of these applications originated outside India. Therein may be found the reason for some of the proposed changes in the patent law.

XIII

Labor Laws and Policies

The peculiar right of labor in India known as bonus was given
legislative sanction in the Payment of Bonus Act, 1965. It was passed
by the Lok Sabha on September 9, 1965, and assented to by the
president on September 25, 1965. The Bonus Act was the final cul-
mination of the 1964 report of the Bonus Commission, but before the
passage of the act, a Bonus Ordinance was issued by the president on
May 31, 1965, enacting temporarily into law the contents of the subsequent act superseding it. The reason given for the hasty implementation of the commission's recommendations, as modified by the government, was that further delay may lead to industrial unrest.

It will be recalled that the commission's report was not unanimous
as the government had hoped. The government's hope was, perhaps,
too sanguine, since one-third of the commission was composed of
members representing workers, one-third representing employers, and
one-third independent. The seventh member, the chairman, M. R.
Mehra, was also presumably independent. N. Dandekar, a retired
I.C.S. who was acting as an independent consultant to business after
retirement, registered a strong dissent on many matters, quite a number of which were adopted by the government in drafting the legislation. It is interesting to note that subsequent to his appointment to the
commission, Mr. Dandekar was elected to Parliament on the Swatan-
tra ticket, which enabled him to participate actively in the passage of
the final act by Parliament.

The commission, first, considered the socio-economic rationale of
the bonus. It found the so-called gap theory—that the *raison d'être*
of the bonus was to close or narrow the gap between the actual wage
and the living wage—difficult to accept. For one thing, the biggest
bonuses have been received in industries already paying the best wages.

Moreover, the gap theory implies that if an industry is able to pay a living wage, it should do so as a wage rather than a bonus.

Its concept of bonus was more prosaic. It concluded, "the concept of bonus is difficult to define in rigid terms, but it is possible to urge that once profits exceed a certain base, labour should legitimately have a share in them. In other words, we think it proper to construe the concept of bonus as sharing by the workers in the prosperity of the concern in which they are employed."[1]

In view of this economic justification, the commission rejected suggestions that the bonus be abolished and replaced with appropriate wage adjustment. Retention of the bonus system, the commission felt, "imparts a measure of desirable flexibility to the wage structure."[2] The workers in India have become habituated to the system and "it suits the workers' pattern of consumption for spending, at least once a year, on some articles of additional and diversified consumption and on needs which cannot be conveniently met from the monthly wage packet."[3] The commission also rejected the suggestion that the bonus be based on production or productivity. It appears that most employers and employers' associations did not favor it.[4]

After concluding that the remedy "is to evolve a satisfactory bonus scheme" that "need not, however, be perfectly logical or aim at giving mathematical justice," the commission sets forth its bonus formula.

To start, *gross profits* are to be determined by adding back to net profit before tax, as per audited profit and loss account, (1) depreciation, (2) development rebate, and (3) other reserves and excluding extraneous profits, such as (a) capital gains and losses, (b) profits and losses from business outside India, (c) profits from investments outside India but only in cases of non-Indian companies, and (d) refund of income taxes paid for previous years.[5]

Prior charges permissible should be the following:

1. Depreciation, computed on the basis of normal depreciation plus multiple shift allowance allowed under the Income Tax Act.[6]

2. Income tax and super tax, but not the super profits tax (replaced in 1965 by the surtax on profits). In determining the charges for income and super tax, the tax reduction on account of development rebate is to be eliminated.[7]

3. Return on capital of 7 per cent and on reserves used as working capital of 4 per cent. The capital should be computed as the net fixed assets plus current assets minus current liabilities.[8]

The gross profits less allowable prior charges leaves the available surplus for allocation between the workers and the company. The commission recommended an allocation formula of 60:40.[9]

Foreign companies that pay the higher 67 per cent income tax are required to allocate 67 per cent of the available surplus for payment of bonus. The commission felt this to be fair since foreign companies will be permitted to deduct taxes at the rate of 67 per cent, as contrasted with 50 per cent for Indian companies, as a prior charge.[10]

The 60 per cent allocation to labor, however, is to be subject to a minimum and maximum bonus.[11] The minimum bonus should be 4 per cent of basic wage and dearness allowance paid during the year or Rs 40, whichever is higher. The maximum bonus should be 20 per cent. In case the minimum exceeds the available surplus in a particular year or the surplus exceeds the maximum, the arrearage or excess (up to a limit of a further 20 per cent) is to be carried forward for appropriate adjustment against future surpluses for four years. The idea of a minimum and maximum bonus is an innovation.

New units, however, should be exempt from bonus payment until the first year of profit, after absorbing accumulated depreciation and previous losses, or the sixth year after the new undertaking begins to sell its products or services, whichever may be earlier.[12]

This comprises basically the Bonus Commission's recommendations. A few more peripheral ones may be noted. Public sector industries, it thought, should be equally liable for bonus payment.[13] The commission also considered whether the bonus formula it proposed should not apply to certain industries. It concluded that the formula should apply to jute, coal, mining, sugar, plantations, tile, cashew, coir, and other industries that pleaded to be exempt for various reasons. The only exceptions made were for banks (where the Desai Award should continue with certain modifications), insurance companies (on account of Section 31A[1] [c] of the Insurance Act), seamen on the high seas, building workers, and small shops employing fewer than twenty persons.[14]

The labor representatives registered some disagreement but no dissent. B. N. Ganguli added a note setting forth some reservations on the application of the bonus scheme to public sector undertakings. N. Dandekar, the industry representative, however, filed a strong note of dissent on the bonus formula recommended by the commission.[15]

Mr. Dandekar urged that the super-profits tax and wealth tax should be allowed as prior charges. His strongest objection, however, was levied at the commission's disallowance of the rehabilitation allowance as a prior charge. In its report, the commission stated that the

40 per cent of the available surplus allocated to the company would enable it to provide for "gratuity and other necessary reserves, the requirements of rehabilitation in addition to the provision made by way of depreciation in the prior charges, the annual provision required, if any, for redemption of debentures and return of borrowings, payment of Super Profits Tax, if any, and additional return on capital."[16] To which Mr. Dandekar replied, "For my part, it seems to me unrealistic to suppose that in the process of meeting this formidable array of obligations out of the retained balance of the available surplus there is likely to be anything left over for rehabilitation."[17]

Mr. Dandekar also recommended that the return on capital should be 8.5 per cent and on reserves 6 per cent, in order to reflect the current situation in the capital and money markets and the increased taxation on investment income. He disagreed with the bonus system on socio-economic grounds but recognized that Indian labor has become habituated to the bonus payments. Hence, he concluded reluctantly, the country will have to live with the system.

Before the introduction of legislation to carry out the Bonus Commission's recommendations, the government made some important changes in the bonus formula. Most notable was the allowance of all direct taxes paid by the company as prior charges. The return on capital was enhanced to 8 per cent on paid up equity capital (7.5 per cent in the case of banks) and 6 per cent on reserves (5 per cent in the case of banks). The return on preference shares, as recommended by the commission, is to be at the actual rate.

To recapitulate, the Bonus Act as finally enacted by Parliament in September, 1965, applies to every factory and every other establishment employing twenty or more people and provides for the payment of bonus in cash within eight months after the close of the accounting year[18] in accordance with the following formula.

1. *Gross profits,* computed per first or second schedule of act, that basically add back depreciation, taxes, and the like and that exclude extraneous profits and losses.[19]
2. *Prior charges,* including,
    (a) Depreciation,[20]
    (b) Development rebate,[21]
    (c) Direct taxes,[22]
    (d) Return on capital,[23]
        (1) Actual rate on preference shares,
        (2) 8 per cent on paid-up equity shares,

(3) 6 per cent on reserves, and,

(4) 7.5 and 5 per cent respectively, in the case of banks.

The remainder, if any, is the *available surplus* allocable 60 per cent (67 per cent in the case of foreign companies) to labor and 40 per cent to the company,[24] subject to a minimum bonus of 4 per cent or Rs 40, whichever is higher, and a maximum bonus of 20 per cent of basic wages and dearness allowance.[25] Any arrearage in the minimum or excess over the maximum up to a further 20 per cent is carried forward for appropriate adjustment against the available surplus for a period of four years.[26] The excess, if any, thereafter belongs to the company.

New establishments are exempt from the payment of bonus until (a) the accounting year in which profits accrue, or (b) the sixth accounting year following the accounting year in which the employer first sells the goods or services, whichever is earlier.[27]

Other notable provisions of the act include its application to public sector enterprises,[28] a limitation of the wages or salaries to Rs 750 per month on which the bonus is computed,[29] forfeiture of bonus by employees dismissed for fraud, theft, misappropriation, or sabotage of any property of the employer and riotous or violent behavior on the premises of the establishment.[30]

A few provisions deal specifically with foreign enterprise. Already mentioned is the higher allocation of 67 per cent of the available surplus in the case of foreign companies not electing to have their dividends taxed in India.[31] The First Schedule, pertaining to banking companies, and the Second Schedule, pertaining to others, exclude profits and losses relating to any business situated outside India and income from investments outside India in the computation of gross profits.[32] The Third Schedule setting forth the allocable return on capital provides that in case of a foreign company within the meaning of Section 591 of the Companies Act, 1956, "the total amount to be deducted . . . shall be 8.5 per cent on the aggregate of the value of the net fixed assets and the current assets of the company in India after deducting the amount of its current liabilities (other than any amount shown as payable to its Head Office whether towards any advance made by the Head Office or otherwise or any interest paid by the Company to its Head Office) in India."[33] Regarding foreign banking companies, the following is provided,

the amount to be deducted under this item shall be the aggregate of—

(i) the dividends payable to its preference shareholders for the accounting year at the rate at which such dividends are payable on such amount as bears the same proportion to its total preference share capital as its total working funds in India bear to its total world working funds;

(ii) 7.5 per cent of such amount as bears the same proportion to its total paid up equity share capital as its total working funds in India bear to its total world working funds;

(iii) 5 per cent of such amount as bears the same proportion to its total disclosed reserves as its total working funds in India bear to its total world working funds. . . .[34]

Section 10 providing for minimum bonus was challenged before the Supreme Court by several companies as unconstitutional because the provision violated Article 14 of the constitution. The argument submitted was that the minimum bonus was payable irrespective of the profits or losses of the companies and that the same burden was imposed on concerns unequally situated. The court upheld the provision.

It would appear that the Bonus Act should bring stability to this area of industrial strife. While the matter of bonus payment remained in the realm of the labor tribunals and courts, it invited controversy and litigation. The act requires both employers and employees to abide by its provisions. Only Parliament can change the bonus formula hereafter. It would appear also that the final bonus formula and limitations are fair to both sides. The employees gained through the provision for minimum bonus, carry forward of minimum bonus deficiency and excess surplus and provision for prompt payment. The employers gained by the 20 per cent limitation on bonus payment and the liberalized prior charges that should enable greater retention of profits for reinvestment or dividends. The private sector owes Mr. Dandekar a vote of thanks for this improved outcome.

XIV

Petroleum and Mineral Rules and Policies

Foreign collaboration has been encouraged and has expanded in the petroleum field the past few years. The Oil India pattern of 51 per cent government control continues as the mode for collaboration in this field.

ESSO entered into 50:50 equity participation with the government for a lube oil plant adjacent to its refinery in Trombay in 1965. In addition, ESSO agreed to use its good offices in the U.S.A. to secure a loan for the balance of the foreign exchange needed in excess of its equity investment. The Madras refinery proposed in collaboration with AMOCO and associates will follow the pattern of the Cochin refinery collaboration with Phillips Petroleum and others, whereby the government will have a 51 per cent controlling equity interest. Both projects, however, are under the effective control of the foreign companies with respect to production and other technical matters.

An interesting development has been the contractual arrangement between ENI of Italy and the government, through the Oil and Natural Gas Commission, for offshore exploration in the Gulf of Cambay. A mobile floating platform with drilling rigs is being supplied on a credit basis under the agreement. Technical assistance and know-how is imparted to ONGC in the difficult art of offshore drilling.

ONGC also secured offshore exploration and production rights in the Persian Gulf from the National Iranian Oil Company. It will undertake the exploration jointly with AGIP of Italy and Phillips of America. A new company will be organized for the purpose, owned 50 per cent by Iranian Oil with the other 50 per cent owned equally by the three foreign collaborators. ONGC's outlay on this venture will entail about $20 million in foreign exchange. Negotiations are presently underway with Kuwait for similar collaboration.

India's concerted effort in this field emanates from a realization that it must secure its petroleum supply to support its pace of industrialization. Indigenous production of crude oil is still woefully short of need despite the development of new sources in Jawalamaki and Cambay in 1957-58. Domestic production is about 5.5 million against consumption of 15 million tons. By 1970 the need is estimated at 27 million tons. Each million tons of crude costs about $12 million; hence, the drive at home and abroad to develop greater crude oil supplies.

In refining, over which a better control can be attained, India expects to be self-sufficient by the end of the Fourth Plan with 22.75 million tons of refining capacity. Eight refineries are either in operation or proposed. The three earliest foreign owned refineries were on stream before 1957. The next three government owned refineries went into production during the period 1962-65. The Cochin and Madras refineries, under the new 51:49 government control pattern, will go into production during the Fourth Plan.

This mixed private and public sector pattern can be expected to continue in India. Any future private collaboration in new refineries will probably have to follow the Cochin pattern. The government prefers foreign collaboration as the wholly owned government refineries have proved more expensive investments per ton of refining capacity. On the other hand, the government is unlikely to sanction refineries that are fully foreign owned as it did in the 1950's.

The government feels the present situation gives it the control it desires over this important industry and yet permits private enterprise to participate. In view of this satisfactory situation there is unlikely to be any nationalization of the three foreign owned refineries in spite of agitation within the country from some quarters for it. It should be noted again that the government is not exactly happy with the refinery agreements, as many in India consider them unfair. The government will, therefore, try to get the harsher terms ameliorated.

In fact, negotiations are already underway with one of the foreign companies, Burmah-Shell, for revision of its agreement. The government would like to have the company include the use of crude produced in India or outside by the government and the use of Indian tankers in connection with the operation of the refinery. Without such cooperation, the foreign owned refineries might find it difficult to obtain sanction for expansion.

A basic change in pricing policy was instituted in early 1966. The import parity formula adopted after the Damle Committee report was considered unfair to the indigenous producers, particularly after the government was able to negotiate discounts on imported crude. This automatically lowered the internal price worked out on the basis of the f.o.b. cost, minus discount, plus freight and insurance. In order to protect and promote the indigenous exploration, production, and refining of oil, the prices of indigenous crude were based on the full f.o.b. prices of analogous crude in the Middle East. At the same time, an import duty of 20 per cent was levied. More precisely, the government resolution reads,

(i) Until further orders, the producers of indigenous crudes will, save in the cases in which a different basis for price fixation may exist under any agreement between the Government and the producer, receive a price that is not less than the landed cost (exclusive of import duty, if any) calculated on the basis of the full posted f.o.b. prices of analogous crudes imported from the Middle East. Users of indigenous crude will be required or requested, as the case may be, to accept this price basis. If and when new circumstances arise; the Government will reconsider the price basis now laid down.

(ii) Ex-refinery prices of bulk refined products in the cases of all refineries in the country, and landed prices, when applicable, will be fixed on the basis of import parity starting from full (i.e., undiscounted) f.o.b. postings at Abadan (at the lowest of Platt's) as on May 18, 1965.

(iii) There will be levied on imported crude a protective import duty at a level determined by the related circumstances prevailing from time to time.

. . . . The decisions herein contained about the prices of oil products will remain in force till December 31, 1967, to begin with, and the Government may extend their validity for a further period or periods.

The government's rationale is found in the following paragraph of the resolution,

The Government has taken particular note of two important factors that have been emerging of late, viz. firstly, the increasing production of crude oil in the country and the growth of indigenous refining capacity based on both local and imported crudes, and secondly, as a consequence, the steady and substantial diminution in the import of finished products and changes in the terms and conditions of such imports. These developments require, among other things, that producers of indigenous crude oil are assured of an adequate price consistent with the costs of exploration and production in the country.

The practice followed hitherto has been to price indigenous crude delivered to the consumer on the basis of parity with the discounted and fluctuating prices of imported crude, from time to time. On crude imports, the Government has been making efforts, with a fair measure of success, to secure prices that are in keeping with world market conditions. The establishment of import prices at fair and reasonable levels is important for the conservation of the country's foreign exchange resources, apart from being justified on purely commercial considerations. The Government will, therefore, continue to work towards this objective with all the means at its disposal, as occasion requires. But in this situation, a modification of the existing practice of pricing indigenous crude is called for, as it does not provide an economic base for the conduct of oil exploration and production operations in the circumstances prevailing in the country. In other words, it is necessary to grant a measure of protection to indigenous crude producers and assure them of a price that is in keeping with the cost of their operations from time to time. Consistent with such crude costs, and in order to maintain the economics of refining operations at reasonable levels, ex-refinery product prices must be re-fixed appropriately. This would not, however, affect the policy of importing products, to the extent imports may be needed, on the best available terms.

The Indian Tariff (Amendment) Ordnance, 1966, was promulgated on February 1, 1966, imposing an import duty of 20 per cent ad valorem on the import of crude petroleum. The duty, more or less, is equal to the discounts India has been getting on the world markets.

The new oil price policy was the outgrowth of the Talukdar Report. This was a working group set up on May 12, 1964, under the secretaryship of J. N. Talukdar, formerly chief secretary of the Government of West Bengal, to advise the government on the proper manner of determining prices of petroleum products. Among other things, the group found that indigenous producers *cum* refiners were unable to operate at a profit under the old formula. The government in promulgating its resolution followed most of the recommendations of the Talukdar working group.

The proposed petro-chemical complexes are an offshoot of the foregoing efforts by India. A $500 million investment is envisaged in this industrial field, during the next two plans. Four petro-chemical complexes are to be set up in Bombay, Gujerat, Haldia, and South India. The products contemplated range from such basic items as carbon black and synthetic rubber to plastics and polyester fibers. Foreign collaboration will be required and the government is encouraging foreign investment in the petro-chemical complexes.

XV

Arbitration

The Supreme Court rendered a significant decision in 1964 on the enforceability of foreign awards in India.[1] The case involved an American company. Since the United States is not a member of the Geneva or United Nations conventions on the recognition and enforcement of foreign arbitral awards, the case had to be decided on English conflict of law principles.

The Supreme Court held that the Indian courts had no jurisdiction to enforce either the foreign arbitration award or a foreign judgment based on the award in the case. Regarding the enforcement of the award the court said,

From all these provisions it would be abundantly clear that the award has no finality till the entire procedure is gone through and that the award as such can never be enforced. There is no provision in the law providing for taking proceedings for the confirmation of an award in which all objections to the award could be made except S. 1461. The proceedings taken thereunder must, however, culminate in a judgment. In this respect, the procedure under the law of the New York State is quite different from that under the Arbitration law of Denmark. Apparently, that is why the plaintiffs, after obtaining the awards, went up to the Supreme Court of New York for obtaining a judgment confirming the awards. No doubt, as a result of the judgment the decision of the arbitrators became unchallengeable in the New York State and for all practical purposes in India as well but in the process the award made by them has given way to the judgment of the Supreme Court of New York. It is this judgment which can now furnish a cause of action to the plaintiffs and not the awards.[2]

But the judgment was also unenforceable. "Since the judgment with which we are concerned was pronounced in New York the cause of action for a suit based thereon must be said to have arisen at that place. Since that is so, it follows that the cause of action in so far as it rests on the judgment, did not arise within the limits of the original jurisdiction of the High Court of Bombay and the suit based upon that judgment must be held to be beyond the jurisdiction of the Court."[3]

The decision concludes that if finality of the award could have been achieved without culminating in a judgment, the award would have been enforceable in India under conflict of law principles. The court concluded that this did not appear possible under New York law.

The report of the Committee on Commercial Arbitration, 1964, is noteworthy. Among other things, the committee recommended that foreign exchange should be made available for Indian companies to participate in arbitration proceedings outside India. Such policy would have the effect of vitiating the basis for the Supreme Court decision in the *Golodetz* case.[4]

Notes

CHAPTER I

1. Woodrow Wyatt, "India on the Move," *The Sunday Times* (London), November 18, 1962, p. 24.

CHAPTER II

1. Memorandum on the Fourth Five-Year Plan, October, 1964, p. 4.
2. *Ibid.*, p. 67-68.
3. Infra, p. 76.

CHAPTER III

1. *Economic Times,* November 30, 1964, October 4, 1965.
2. *Economic Times,* January 1, 1966.

CHAPTER IV

1. The Land Acquisition (Companies) Rules, 1963, Rule 3.
2. *Ibid.*, Rule 4.
3. *Ibid.*, Rule 4(2), Explanation.
4. *Ibid.*, Rule 5.
5. *Ibid.*, Rule 8.
6. The Land Acquisition Act, 1894, Sec. 44A.

CHAPTER VI

1. Indira Gandhi, "India Today: A Program for a Planned Democracy," 50 *The Yale Review*, 321, 325.
2. See the *New York Times,* January 27, 1966.
3. Supra, p. 5, *et seq*.
4. *Report of the Monopolies Inquiry Commission,* 1965, p. i.
5. *Ibid.*, pp. 136-37.
6. *Ibid.*, pp. 7-8.
7. *Ibid.*, p. 200.

8. See Matthew J. Kust, *Foreign Enterprise in India: Laws and Policies* (Chapel Hill: The University of North Carolina Press, 1964), p. 140. Hereinafter cited as text.

9. *Report of the Monopolies Inquiry Commission*, 1965, p. 203.

10. *Ibid.*, p. 142.

11. *Ibid.*, p. 201.

12. *Ibid.*, p. 163.

13. *Ibid.*, p. 199.

14. *Ibid.*, p. 160.

15. *Ibid.*, p. 163.

16. *Ibid.*, p. 164.

17. There have been four surveys to date to be found in the following issues: August 5, 1963; February 10, 1964; November 30, 1964; and October 4, 1965.

18. See *Economic Times*, November 5, 1965.

19. See text, p. 179.

20. See *Economic Times*, November 14, 1965.

CHAPTER VII

1. *Report of Monopolies Inquiry Commission*, 1965, p. 143.

2. See text, p. 209-10.

3. See *Handbook of Export Promotion*, 1965, Appendix 31.

4. *Ibid.*, p. 5.

CHAPTER VIII

1. See Statement of the Finance Minister, *Economic Times*, December 4, 1964.

2. Foreign Exchange Regulation Act, 1947, as amended, Sec. 25 A.

3. *Ibid.*, Sec. 19A, 19H.

4. *Ibid.*, Sec. 19J.

5. *Ibid.*, Sec. 27(2) (c).

6. *Ibid.*, Sec. 5(1) (aa) 6a. *Ibid.*, Sec. 13(4) (6).

7. *Ibid.*, Sec. 13(4) (c).

8. *Ibid.*, Sec. 17.

9. *Ibid.*, Sec. 18(3C).

10. *Ibid.*, Sec. 18B.

11. *Exchange Control Manual*, 5th ed., p. 33.

12. *Ibid.*, p. 33.

13. *Ibid.*, p. 45.

14. *Ibid.*, p. 109.

CHAPTER IX

1. *Report of the Commission of Inquiry* (of Dalmia-Jain Companies), 1963.

2. *Report of the Commission of Inquiry on The Administration of Dalmia-Jain Companies*, April 23, 1963.

3. Notification G.S.R. No. 178, February 1, 1964.
4. *Ninth Annual Report,* p. 23.
5. See text, pp. 392-93.
6. The Companies Act, 1956, as amended, Sec. 209(d).
7. *Ibid.,* Sec. 209(4A).
8. *Ibid.,* Sec. 209(4).
9. *Ibid.,* Sec. 209(6) (a).
10. *Ibid.,* Sec. 227(1A).
11. *Ibid.,* Sec. 227(4A).
12. *Ibid.,* Sec. 233B.
13. *Ibid.,* Sec. 259.
14. *Ibid.,* Sec. 264(2).
15. *Ibid.,* Sec. 314.
16. *Seventh Annual Report . . . year ending March 31, 1963,* p. 24.
17. *Ibid.,* p. 24.
18. *Ibid.,* p. 24-25.
19. *Ninth Annual Report . . . year ending March 31, 1965,* p. 27.
20. *Seventh Annual Report . . . year ending March 31, 1963,* pp. 28-29.
21. *Eighth Annual Report . . . year ending March 31, 1964,* p. 15.
22. *Ninth Annual Report . . . year ending March 31, 1965,* pp. 24-25.
23. *Eighth Annual Report . . . year ending March 31, 1964,* p. 17.
24. *Report of the Monopolies Inquiry Commission, 1965,* p. 188.
25. *Ibid.,* pp. 191-92.
26. *Economic Times,* November 8, 1964.
27. *Seventh Annual Report . . . year ending March 31, 1963,* p. 27-28.
28. The Companies Act, 1956, as amended, Sec. 294(5).
29. *Ibid.,* Sec. 294(6).
30. *Ibid.,* Sec. 294(4).
31. *Ibid.,* Sec. 294A.
32. See text, p. 304.
33. *The Report of the Monopolies Commission, 1965,* p. 186-88.
34. *Ibid.,* p. 205.
35. *Kalinga Tubes, Ltd. v. Shanti Prasad Jain et al.,* A.I.R. (1963) Orissa 189.
36. *Murhalidhar Jhunjhanwala, et al. v. Sindri Iron Foundry(p), Ltd.* (1964) 34 Comp. Cas. 510.
37. *Asoka Cement Private, Ltd. and Rameshwar Dayal Dobey v. Kamika Mukherji, et al.,* an unreported decision of the Calcutta High Court, March 22, 1963.
38. See *Murhalidhar case* (above, n. 36).
39. The Companies Act, 1956, as amended, Sec. 394(1) (b), Provisos.
40. *Ibid.,* Sec. 395.

CHAPTER XI

1. The Finance Act, 1966, First Schedule, Part I.
2. Indian Income Tax Act, 1961, as amended, Sec. 104-9.
3. *Ibid.,* Sec. 104(4) (c).
4. The Finance Act, 1966, First Schedule.

5. Indian Income Tax Act, 1961, as amended, Sec. 45; see also Finance Act, 1961, Sec. 13.

6. See Finance Act, 1966, Sec. 43(b).

7. *Ibid.*, First Schedule, Part I, Para. F., II.

8. Indian Income Tax Act, 1961, as amended, Sec. 85B, 85C.

9. Companies (Profits) Surtax Act, Third Schedule, Sec. (1) (iii).

10. Indian Income Tax Act, 1961, as amended, Sec. 80E.

11. *Ibid.*, Sec. 33A.

12. *Ibid.*, Sec. 33A(a), (b).

13. The Finance Act, 1965, Sec. 2(5) (a).

14. Indian Income Tax Act, 1961, as amended, Sec. 54A.

15. *Ibid.*, Sec. 10 (4A).

16. *Ibid.*, Sec. 10(6) (ix).

17. *Ibid.*, Sec. 10(6) (vii).

18. *Ibid.*, Sec. 280Z.

19. *Ibid.*, Sec. 280ZA.

20. *Ibid.*, Sec. 280ZB.

21. *Ibid.*, Sec. 280D.

22. Notification G.S.R. No. 1636, November 5, 1965.

23. Indian Income Tax Act, 1961, Sec. 280ZC.

24. Notification G.S.R. No. 1183, August 17, 1965.

25. Indian Income Tax Act, 1961, as amended, Sec. 84.

26. *Ibid.*, Sec. 35A.

27. Wealth Tax Act, Sec. 5(1) (xx).

28. Finance Act, 1965, First Schedule, Parts I and II.

29. Indian Income Tax Act, 1961, as amended, Sec. 10(ix).

30. *Ibid.*, Sec. 10(x).

31. *Ibid.*, Sec. 87A.

32. Budget 1966-67, Finance Minister's Speech (Part B), p. 2.

CHAPTER XII

1. *The Gazette of India,* No. 42, Sept. 25, 1965, p. 958.

2. *Report on the Revision of the Patents Law, 1959,* pp. 37-42.

3. *Ibid.*, p. 37.

4. *Ibid.*, pp. 24-37.

CHAPTER XIII

1. *Report of the Bonus Commission, 1964,* p. 19.

2. *Ibid.*, p. 107.

3. *Ibid.*

4. *Ibid.*, pp. 23-27.

5. *Ibid.*, pp. 38-40.

6. *Ibid.*, pp. 41-42.

7. *Ibid.*, pp. 42-43.

8. *Ibid.*, pp. 55-56.

9. *Ibid.*, pp. 55-56.

10. *Ibid.*, p. 43.

11. *Ibid.*, p. 56.
12. *Ibid.*, p. 57.
13. *Ibid.*, pp. 57, 88-89.
14. *Ibid.*, pp. 60-87.
15. *Ibid.*, pp. 97-106.
16. *Ibid.*, p. 55.
17. *Ibid.*, p. 100.
18. The Payment of Bonus Act, 1965, Sec. 19.
19. *Ibid.*, Sec. 4, First and Second Schedules.
20. *Ibid.*, Sec. 6(a).
21. *Ibid.*, Sec. 6(b).
22. *Ibid.*, Sec. 6(c), 7.
23. *Ibid.*, Sec. 6(a), Third Schedule.
24. *Ibid.*, Sec. 2(4).
25. *Ibid.*, Sec. 10, 11.
26. *Ibid.*, Sec. 15.
27. *Ibid.*, Sec. 16.
28. *Ibid.*, Sec. 20.
29. *Ibid.*, Sec. 12.
30. *Ibid.*, Sec. 9.
31. *Ibid.*, Sec. 2(4) (a).
32. *Ibid.*, First Schedule, 3(e), 6(b), 6(c), Second Schedule, 3(e), 6(b), 6(c).
33. *Ibid.*, Third Schedule, 1, Proviso.
34. *Ibid.*, Third Schedule, 2, Proviso.

CHAPTER XV

1. *Badat & Co. v. East India Trading Co.*, A.I.R. (1964) S. C. 538.
2. *Ibid.*, 558-59.
3. *Ibid.*, 555.
4. See text, p. 463.

Index

www.ingramcontent.com/pod-product-compliance
Lightning Source LLC
Chambersburg PA
CBHW021603210326
41599CB00010B/582